THE RULES
OF LAWFUL
BEHAVIOR

THE RULES OF LAWFUL BEHAVIOR

Understanding American Law Through the Examination of 20 Human Behaviors, Including Analysis of the Behavioral and Legal Aspects of Some Recent High Profile Cases like Andy Lopez, Oscar Grant, Michael Brown, Trayvon Martin, and Others.

JOHN R. BELLANCA

DORRANCE PUBLISHING CO
EST. 1920
PITTSBURGH, PENNSYLVANIA 15238

I'd like to dedicate this book to Generations Y and Z, and to generations to come not yet named—*they need this the most*. While redemption from our behavior is possible, it would be nice if we knew a thing or two *before* we face the situations that we will ultimately need redemption from!

*　*　*

(And can we please start coming up with better names for future generations? X, Y, and Z seem so final. The lettering system is useful in that it is a generic name for a generation (about a 20-30 year time span) before any attributes become dominant enough to give a nickname to its members, and the nickname for Generation Y has definitely become "Millennials." Yes, it all started with the unknowns and mysteries surrounding Generation X, a generation I was at first on the cusp of, but now have been designated as belonging to as the times and historical events have unfolded. But to continue on alphabetically from X with only two generations left to the end of the alphabet was a huge mistake—it only feeds into the bullshit that end times are upon us with Z being the last generation. The easiest thing to do moving forward would be to just reset back to A as the generic name for the generation following Z (which has already started), but I believe we need a different generic naming system of some sort. How about using 'M3G01'for the generic name for the first generation of the 3rd Millennium of the Gregorian Calendar? Or just G1 for short. Then, numerically from there, G2, G3, G4, etc. instead of using letters of the alphabet. It is a good time to start a new naming convention as G1 would be the first generation of the millennium after the Millennials. Generation Z becomes G1—the first generation, not the last.)

TABLE OF CONTENTS

INTRODUCTION

The reason why this book hasn't already been written by someone else is because no one wants to acknowledge what has become painfully obvious: That the law has become the moral code of American Culture.

The law is the lowest common denominator of right and wrong. People don't ask any more if something is right or wrong, they ask if something is legal or illegal. What is legal becomes right and what is illegal becomes wrong—without consideration of the morality of the behavior.

Traditional institutions of morality (churches, synagogues, temples and mosques) are now irrelevant enough to enough people; or are contradictory enough either with each other or with modern notions of justice and science; or they are just considered supplemental to modern day life by enough people that they are no longer the principle sayers and keepers of 'what's right' and 'what's wrong.' It is the lawfulness of any behavior that is now the central question.

But we generally don't spend our Sunday mornings learning about the greatness of the law. We don't dress up, gather together, and sing songs of joy to the law. But, maybe we should?!? After all, American Law is based on a rich tradition known as the Common Law, (the law that 'started about a thousand years ago in the Middle Ages in England to bring consistency to legal proceedings throughout the land where traditional Christian principles and customs were adhered to in order to achieve a sense of justice'—definitional verbiage borrowed and consolidated from Wikipedia). It is all of the legal decisions that are found in court documents and court cases throughout the last thousand years or so, and later cases either uphold or reverse earlier decisions that reflect changing societal values. From this, we now have time tested principles that form a body of law that is still growing and changing to accommodate the challenges of today's technological and globalized world. This is the law that our forefathers embraced and brought with them to our nation. It is the law of free people.

But, of course, American Law is not only the Common Law—it is much bigger (as if a thousand years of decisions weren't enough) with laws being regularly added and changed by acts of our government and by referendum (ballot measures). And, there are differing layers of jurisdictions (a designation of legal authority, usually understood as local, state, and federal jurisdictions) where there may be differences in what is considered lawful behavior. There are models of law created and published by institutions and nonprofit organizations that are adopted, in whole or in part, by different jurisdictions, and there are an awful lot of binding procedural rules in place everywhere. There are our founding documents (the Declaration of Independence and the Constitution with our Bill of Rights), the Uniform Code of Military Justice, the body of Maritime Law, and a host of international treaties signed and adopted which make up a nebulous web of International Law.

The funny thing is that no matter how complex or how big the law gets, it all seems to circle back to a core set of human behaviors that are found within the Common Law (more broadly stated as Traditional Law or Case Law). Concerns about this core set of human behaviors crosses jurisdictional lines, bodies of law, international boundaries, generations, and most religious beliefs.

This book is an overview of those behaviors, expressing pretty much all of the fundamentals of American law in 20 human behaviors. Believe in whatever else you want, subscribe to any way of life that feels right for you, and follow whatever faith that speaks to you—these are some of the fundamental privileges we have living as free people—but the information inside of this book is what you need to know in order to live a lawful life in a free country.

Congratulations! You have been born into, came to, or are visiting a free country. You should use this book as a guide for how to behave while you are here.

THE RULES OF LAWFUL BEHAVIOR

TEN FORBIDDEN BEHAVIORS

All Traditional Law stems from the Golden Rule, *"Do unto others as you would have them do unto you."* This ancient philosophical law of reciprocity appears in some form or another in all religious teachings. Under Traditional Western Common Law, there is an inference of harm to another if you break the Golden Rule, and any behavior that leads to an articulated harm becomes against the law, illegal, or unlawful (this book uses the more general term *unlawful* because to say something is illegal implies a specific violation of a specific law based on specific facts). Behaviors that lead to these articulated harms are therefore forbidden. There are ten forbidden behaviors, as follows:

FIGURE 1. TEN FORBIDDEN BEHAVIORS

Behavior by Number	Forbidden Behavior	Resulting Criminal Charge or Civil Claim
1	**No Bullying** (Acts of non-physical aggression such as intimidation, harassment, or other threatening behavior)	Assault / Intentional Infliction of Emotional Distress / Defamation / Invasion of Privacy / Hate Crimes / Stalking / Criminal Harassment / Discrimination / etc. (***Et cetera,*** because the violation could have any number of names given by a legislative body at any level of government.)
2	**No Hitting or Touching** (Acts of physical aggression or using a weapon to hurt someone)	Battery / Mayhem / Statutory Assault / Aggravated Assault / etc.
3	**No Killing**	Any Degree of Murder / Manslaughter / Criminal Homicide / Wrongful Death / etc.
4	**No Forcing Anyone to Go Somewhere or Do Something Against Their Will**	Kidnapping / False Imprisonment / Coercion / etc.
5	**No Forcing or Tricking Anyone to Engage in a Sexual Act**	Rape / Statutory Rape / Indecency / Lewd and Lascivious Acts / Solicitation / etc.

6	**No Going Anywhere You Aren't Supposed To Go**	Trespassing / Burglary / Breaking and Entering / etc.
7	**No Taking Property or Keeping Property You Know Belongs to Someone Else**	Larceny / Robbery / Extortion / Embezzlement / Larceny by Trick / False Pretenses / Conversion / Receiving Stolen Property / Theft / Piracy / Fraud / etc.
8	**No Destroying / Burning Other People's Property**	Trespass to Chattel / Vandalism / Arson / etc.
9	**No Making Plans with Anyone to Do Anything Unlawful, No Asking Anyone Else to Do Anything Unlawful, No Attempting to Do Anything Unlawful, and No Helping Anyone Else After They Do Something Unlawful**	Solicitation / Conspiracy / Accomplice Liability / Aiding and Abetting / Accessory before-the-fact / Attempt (of a crime) / Accessory after-the-fact / Harboring a Fugitive / Racketeering / Charges under RICO (for organized crime) / etc.
10	**No Breaking Your Promises**	Breach of Contract (when your promises constitute a contract, and the civil liability that would follow)

NO BULLYING

While bullying is somewhat considered to be not that serious of an offense by many, it is the all-important very first step of unlawful behavior where one feels emboldened enough to act in such a way that their will (one's determination, desire, intent, or purpose of action) somehow supersedes or may otherwise impose upon the will of another.

It is a delicate balance we all must find in our lives, where we come to know ourselves and compete in this world to become the best we can be, finding our talents, exploring our gifts, becoming who we ultimately will be, AND to acknowledge our boundaries where our rights end and the rights of others begin, to know that others get to compete in this world alongside us and become the best *they* can be, finding *their* talents, exploring *their* gifts, becoming who *they* will ultimately become—WITHOUT ANY INTERFERENCE FROM US.

While we are only now starting to take a hard look at the behavior of bullying as a society, it is the term "bullying" that is so fitting to describe this vague and unclear behavior that everyone seems to know, but there is no universal definition that seems to cover all of it.

What we do agree upon is that bullying comes in many forms, and it is hard to draw bright line rules of exact prohibited behavior. Clearly, if there is a physical harm, a wrong has been committed. But just when does teasing, assertion of strength, or recognition of differences become bullying? Is it an objective standard that can be defined, or is it by the subjective feelings one feels when the spotlight is upon them? Does a behavior need to cause a certain level of harm before it is considered bullying? Does a behavior have to be repeated a certain number of times, or require a certain amount of force before it is considered bullying?

Regardless of precise definition, bullying occurs when natural boundaries are crossed, and there is interference with the natural rights of others. It is hard to defend a bully. No one likes a bully. When someone feels entitled enough to impose their will onto others—and does so regularly and freely—they are not only a bully, but they are well on their way to becoming a criminal if they do not learn to control their impulses. Bullying is truly a slippery slope (the idea that one thing quickly leads to another in a negative way). If we recognize bullying simply as the human behavior of violating personal boundaries and interfering with the natural rights of others, then we have articulated our first forbidden behavior.

It is imperative each of us discover and understand our own personal boundaries as soon as we can, and to teach others, (especially children) to do the same. Otherwise, we run the risk of behaving in such a way that violates the natural rights of others, and:

- If you do so in such a way that there is the fear of an imminent threat (usually by attempting some sort of violence) you will be committing the crime of Common Law Assault.

- If you do it to cause fear, and there is fear, you will be committing the intentional tort of Assault (a tort is a civil wrong settled in civil court between the involved parties, as opposed to a crime for which you are tried in criminal court by the charging jurisdiction, which is usually the state where you live).

- If what you do is so extreme and outrageous that it would be considered outside the bounds of decency, and it causes someone severe emotional distress, you will be committing the tort of Intentional Infliction of Emotional Distress.

- If you disseminate false or untrue information about someone that causes harm to their reputation (like spreading a rumor), you will be committing Defamation.

- If you disclose details about someone's personal life (especially if you snoop) and you embarrass them, you are probably committing one of the Invasion of Privacy torts.

- If you follow someone around, or otherwise won't leave them alone, you are probably stalking or harassing them.

- If you pick on certain groups of people, especially with others, you may be committing hate crimes and violating discrimination laws.

- And if someone dies, your bullying will probably show premeditation, demonstrate malice, or show criminal intent, allowing for maximum penalties in the law for a death you may not have ever in your wildest dreams think would occur.

You could spend a lot of time and energy learning all the boundaries and intricacies of all of these laws and others specific to certain jurisdictions or circumstances so you can avoid legal liability for your bad behavior—some people do just that so they can get away with as much bullying as they can and still fall short of incurring liability (I used to have a douchebag friend who would do shit like that). The key, though, is to understand that forbidden behavior starts with the idea that it is okay to impose your will onto others, to cross natural boundaries, and to interfere with the natural rights of others—it is not okay. To simplify: _No Bullying_.

NOTE: An act of bullying is essentially an act of harassment, and vice-versa. But the word 'harassment' carries with it connotations of specific wrongdoings because there are crimes and torts called harassment, like sexual harassment. In order to distinguish and describe this behavior outside of any preconceived notions, and be more inclusive regarding the outward nature of the behavior, I am using the word bullying. Again, everyone knows what a bully is.

LEGAL NOTE: I can see in the near future that a universal definition of bullying will probably develop. It will probably develop out of current legal principles from the torts of Negligence, Trespass, and Nuisance, where the violation comes from unreasonable, repeated, or continued behavior with knowledge and notice, with the _mens rea_ (Latin for 'guilty mind', which has come to mean one's mental state or frame of mind at the time of an act) being that one knew or should have known of an inevitable harm. If I may be so bold as to offer that definition, it would be something to the effect of, "Any unreasonable behavior that violates the personal boundaries of another, thereby interfering with their natural rights causing harm." Then, actual cases would define the boundaries of acceptable behavior and the requisite level of harm that would need to be shown based on reasonableness (Reasonableness is discussed as Behavior 13). Criminal liability would follow with certain levels of harm and intent. As this is not specifically the law now, it would have to be introduced by a legislative body, voted in by referendum, or created through judge-made law (which can be controversial because judges really aren't supposed to proactively legislate from the bench or make new laws when rendering a decision—they have to enforce the law by following what was decided before by previous courts through a principle known as *stare decisis*), but the reality is that a decision has to be made for any new matter before a court, which is referred to as a matter of first impression.

NO HITTING OR TOUCHING

Hitting or touching can be seen as the logical progression of bullying, where the exertion of one's will becomes physical in nature. Only with hitting or touching, the violation is easier to define than with bullying as the law specifically protects the bodily integrity of others. You can, and will probably be, arrested and/or sued if you go around hitting or touching people without their permission (see Behavior 14 about Consent/Permission).

If you hit or touch another:

- And it is offensive, or out of anger, or in retribution (whether or not you cause injury): It is a crime, and you can be arrested and prosecuted by the charging jurisdiction for the crime.

- Intentionally: It is a tortious act, and you can be sued for damages by the victim just because you hit or touched them as damages are generally presumed when you hit or touch someone. You can also face criminal charges for the same act! It would not be considered double jeopardy (being tried twice for the same act) because a crime is charged by the jurisdiction in criminal court and damages are sought by the victim in civil court.

- Accidentally, and you were negligent (acting unreasonably, see Behavior 13) and caused someone to be injured: It is a tortious act, and you can be sued by the victim for their injuries. Depending on the level of your negligence and the amount of harm you cause, you can also face criminal charges for your negligence.

And when you hit or touch someone, it generally doesn't matter why you hit or touched them—only that you hit or touched them, or your actions led to them being hit or touched (either criminally, intentionally, or negligently). And, hitting or touching someone with an object or indirectly is the same thing as hitting them directly. Unless your behavior is justified when you hit or touched someone because you defended yourself, someone else, or your property (see Behaviors 17-19 for Justified Behaviors), or you have their consent to hit or touch them (see Behavior 14 about Consent/Permission), you may never hit or touch anyone. And here is the icing on the cake: Not even if they deserve it! It was in this context in which my mother taught me as a small boy that "two wrongs do not make a right." Admittedly, I was a bit easily provoked in my youth. (See Behavior 17 for a discussion about fighting).

NOTE: *No Bullying* and *No Hitting or Touching* in the law are called Assault and Battery, and are good examples of the evolution of the law and how the law changes over time. Assault and Battery used to be separate and distinct offenses in criminal law. But, over time, these offenses have become conflated into one notion in many jurisdictions because the exact behavior of the perpetrator might overlap or support a charge for only one of the offenses, while the intent or injuries might support a charge for the other in certain circumstances—and some offenders either escaped liability or incurred greater liability based on inconsistent case law precedent. Efforts of simplification led to codification (an articulation of the law, usually found in a legal code). But, the law didn't evolve exactly the same way everywhere, and there are small differences in what Assault and Battery mean in different jurisdictions, and what exact behavior constitutes either Assault and/or Battery. But just because the name or the intent of the behavior became articulated in some particular way, the protection of bodily integrity has not changed. It is the protected liberty of bodily integrity that endures regardless of any codified definition.

ADDITIONAL NOTE: There are more justifications in the law than what are being mentioned here that will allow someone to touch another, including justifications for law enforcement and the appropriate discipline of children (See Section 4 for more information on Justified Behaviors). However, this is a discussion about the Rules of Lawful Behavior, not the *exceptions* to the Rules of Lawful Behavior, and the rule is <u>you may never hit or touch anyone</u>.

WARNING: If your focus is on the exceptions to the Rules of Lawful Behavior, you may be a douchebag.

NO KILLING

FOR FUCK'S SAKE! DO YOU REALLY NEED TO BE TOLD NOT TO KILL ANYONE? If you can't mess with people (no bullying,) or smack them around (no hitting or touching,) you certainly can't kill them! Again, FOR FUCK'S SAKE!

"THOU SHALL NOT KILL" is one of the 10 Commandments written by the finger of God and delivered to Moses IN STONE! Murder is the highest of unlawful offenses and is the most seriously punished of offenses today as the law recognizes that any one person's right to live their life is no different than any other person's right to live *their* life. It is beyond me how anyone could not understand this fundamental Rule of Lawful Behavior.

Yet, American culture is completely saturated with the image of killing. It's everywhere. Constantly. One could even say we are obsessed with killing. Graphic depictions of killing and death permeate our daily lives on TV, in movies, on the internet, and now, we even simulate graphic realistic killing in video games. "I'm going to kill you!" is such a common expression, it now only means you are angry with someone.

And if anyone thinks I'm exaggerating about the video games, do yourself a favor and go online and search for Grand Theft Auto, and watch some videos of the characters you can play. You can drive drunk, run from police, beat up prostitutes, run over homeless people, torture suspected terrorists, and, of course, kill whoever you want. I won't play that game or others like it: I don't want to know what it feels like to intentionally target and kill someone, or run them over with a car, or beat them up with a club. I don't want to plot and scheme inside such a game to somehow advance myself by doing that kind of shit, and I especially don't want that shit showing up in my dreams or coming to mind as I'm waking up. I don't think the warning label on those types of video games is strong enough—they should say that acting out violence can change a person, even haunt a person, especially those who are impressionable—like young kids who are going through pretty dramatic physical, hormonal, and emotional changes almost daily as it is already. I don't want to come off like one of those prudish *"What about the children"* {said in a high, hysterical, *Simpson's-episode* voice} types, but what exactly are we teaching the next generations? Some level of innocence needs to be protected because you cannot unring a bell or unsee violence. Of course, it is not possible to go through life wearing rose-colored glasses, thinking life is nothing but wonderfulness. BUT DAAAAMN! It's another thing entirely when people embrace violence and simulate it every day for hours on end. If GTA and first-person shooter video games are your thing, just be aware of the Law of Attraction that says "like energies attract." Some people believe that you can actually bring different kinds of energies into your life just by focusing on them—just read or watch *The Secret*. I'm still waiting for the technology of the first-person shooter experience to become the first-person virtual reality experience where we buy vacation package cartridges for our home game consoles.

Throughout the eons of existence, killing has always been seen as wrongful. And no matter how much our culture seems to want to normalize the act of killing, whether it be for honor, duty, protection, or whatever—it is fundamentally wrong to kill. Of course, there are exceptions and justifications, but the rule is <u>No Killing</u>. (See Section 4 for more information on Justified Behaviors.)

NOTE ABOUT KILLING ANIMALS: While I deplore hunting and fishing for sport, I do applaud the hunter's credo of *"Don't kill it unless you plan to eat it."* I am a carnivore, and like most people, I love a good steak! However, I prefer to remain far removed from the details of how yummy stuff makes it to my dinner plate. It's a sort of willful blindness to the obvious fact that we are all part of the food chain and the cycle of life. I fully respect the farmers of every kind who provide the bounty of food found at my local grocery store, and I'll absolutely cook and eat fish I catch—an invaluable lesson in self-sufficiency and the value of life my father taught me growing up. But if killing is simply for the joy and amusement of killing, I extend the rule of *No Killing* to animals and nature. If someone is killing animals for the joy and amusement of killing, they are a piece of shit who needs psychiatric help. Further, you don't need to kill anything to know how to use a weapon. I qualified as an expert marksman when I wore the uniform of a soldier during peacetime, and I've never had to kill anyone or anything. I fully support the conservation and preservation of all life, with all harvesting always being sustainable ... I think God would have wanted it that way.

NO FORCING ANYONE TO GO SOMEWHERE OR DO SOMETHING AGAINST THEIR WILL

So far, the rules of lawful behavior have addressed the relationship between one person's individual natural rights and another person's individual natural rights (a battle of wills or *mano-a-mano*). This next rule, however, touches upon the relationship between an individual and our society at large—considering our rights, freedoms, and liberties as Americans.

The journey each of us has before us so that we may fully realize our freedom and liberty, starts with our understanding that freedom and liberty start with <u>freedom of movement</u>. We may pretty much go anywhere we want, any time we wish, unhindered and unencumbered. We may certainly travel on public roads anywhere within our communities, cities, states, and all of the United States with very little restrictions or limitations. No one may hinder our free movement or imprison us without cause and due process under the law. If they do, we have the right to petition the federal government to make them stop—known as a *writ of habeas corpus*—one of the most quintessential elements of a free society.

Additionally, our country was founded upon the principles of natural law (the philosophy that we inherit our rights from God or nature, not from some king or government).

SO WHAT IN THE HELL WOULD MAKE YOU THINK THAT YOUR IN-DIVIDUAL WILL AND PERSONAL DESIRE COULD EVER ALLOW YOU TO INFRINGE UPON SOMEONE ELSE'S GOD GIVEN FREEDOM AND LIBERTY?

<u>You may not control the freedom of movement of another.</u> If you do, you will be committing the crime of Kidnapping or False Imprisonment. And this should go without saying, but you especially may not control the freedom of movement of another as a means to an end to commit a crime! Additionally, if you force others to behave in a certain way, anything they do on your behalf is the same thing as you doing it directly—that is called *coercion*.

A NOTE ABOUT NATURAL LAW: It is important to note that traditionally, American law has always been about the protection of our natural rights and the protection of the autonomy of the individual. The goal of American law has always been to protect us from the unlawful acts of others, not to establish some authoritarian code of conduct that could somehow infringe upon our natural freedoms.

NO FORCING OR TRICKING ANYONE TO ENGAGE IN A SEXUAL ACT

Rape is most heinous because it is the ultimate collision between one's will (the forcer) and another's freedom and liberty (the forcee). There is no greater license of one's will, nor a more intimate violation of another's personal freedom, liberty, or bodily integrity.

At the most basic level, nothing more needs to be said: <u>You may only copulate with another with their permission/consent.</u>

See Behavior 14 for a general discussion about Consent/Permission, and below for a discussion about consent specifically regarding participation in a sexual act:

First things first: Keep in mind that one can only legally give consent for participation in a sexual act if they have reached the age of consent for such participation, which varies state by state and is between 16 and 18 years old. If you disregard this aspect of consent, you will probably be charged with Statutory Rape (any sexual act with someone below the age of consent is automatically considered rape by law, or by 'statute'). If both parties are below the age of consent, each case is decided individually, and criminality of the act(s) is decided based on the age and maturity of each child in what is known as prosecutorial discretion.

The key to navigating our complex sexual culture today is to fully understand the concept of consent. The direction the law now seems to be moving is to focus on the consent you have for any sexual act, rather than on the nature of the act, where the law seems to be less concerned with what you do and how you do it, and far more concerned that you have the permission/consent from those you do it with.

And yes, the law used to be very concerned with what you did and how you did it. There have been all kinds of efforts throughout our history to impose moral codes that have largely failed over time. And the definitions of acceptable sexual behavior continue to evolve. We have seen The Sexual Revolution that started in the 1960's, The Gay Liberation Movement with an ongoing LGBTQ+ Revolution, and there is now the general acceptance of sexual fantasy and the explosion of sexually explicit material now widely available EVERYWHERE! What was once suppressed and kept private not very long ago is now very much out in the open, and we now even share intimate photos of ourselves on social media. Many people seem to be seeking permissions that exceed what is traditionally understood as our inalienable rights of "life, liberty, and the pursuit of happiness."

But this is the era of #MeToo (the social media hashtag where people share their stories of sexual abuse), where, if nothing else, we have learned just how many people have been victims of sexual misconduct of one kind or another. Now more than ever, it needs to be stated clearly and without any ambiguity— you need the permission/consent from your partner(s) before engaging in any sexual act, any intimate or friendly touching, or any intimate imposition of personal space.

This has become such an area of focus that many colleges and universities have addressed the issue by creating codes of conduct and policy guidelines on the need for consent, while states and other jurisdictions grapple with legislation to strengthen sexual misconduct laws.

There is a growing Affirmative Consent Movement where the slogan is "Yes Means Yes," and the standard is that you must obtain the affirmative permission of your partner(s) before engaging in any sexual activity. According to the movement, silence does not mean yes, not saying "No" does not mean yes, and only "Yes" means yes. And that makes perfect sense! After all, if "No" means no, shouldn't "Yes" mean yes? And, if you don't know for sure, shouldn't you clarify which it is?

But the Affirmative Consent Movement is not without its problems. What if getting an affirmative "Yes" is ever overlooked? How many times do we find ourselves in a situation of intimacy where we don't actually know where it is going to end up? An intimate situation where hand holding may lead to an embrace, maybe even a kiss, some touching, or even more. When _exactly_ is it appropriate to get the affirmative permission of your partner not only for where the situation may lead, but for the intimate touching of a sexual nature that has already occurred? At what point _exactly_ has one crossed some line and has acted without the affirmative consent of their partner, which may lead to serious charges or claims against them for inappropriate behavior? And, is someone in the clear if they get a "Yes" after-the-fact?

The issue with legislating a requirement for obtaining the affirmative consent of your sexual partner(s) is this: 'Is the law going to impose a _duty to act_ regarding sexual behavior?' A duty to act is when the law requires you to do something. Generally, American law does not require you to do much of anything. The only time the law requires you to do something is when certain criteria are met and the law imposes conditions, like you have to get a drivers' license and follow the rules of the road in order to drive on public roads—but there are no laws that say you have to drive a car. In fact, you never really have to do anything except file your taxes or register for Selective Service (the draft). The question here is, "Will the law require us (or establish a duty) to get the affirmative consent (get a "Yes") from our sexual partner(s) before _any act_ which could be seen as sexual in nature in order for our behavior to not be considered unlawful?"

Actually, I would argue that there is already an _implied duty to act_ with regard to sexual behavior, and the law simply acknowledges a narrow window of compliance. And compliance with this implied duty lies in the communication between the partners. Through their verbal and non-verbal communication, each partner grants and receives a sort of step-by-step consent with each new level of intimacy through a process of what could be understood as Continuing Consent (a system of consent that has been recognized in the medical field where there is an ongoing consent after the initial informed consent throughout a medical treatment). Our parents and grandparents would have described this idea of step-by-step consent using a baseball metaphor: "Susie and Bob were necking and Susie let Bob get to third base, but she said no when he went for a home run." Bob has always had a duty to seek Susie's consent for each new level of intimacy, and Susie has always had the ability to grant or deny her consent each step along the way—even if Susie was super kinky and she gave her permission for everything in the _Kama_

Sutra, Susie could always say no at any time to any specific act or call the whole thing off.

There are other models of consent that also acknowledge non-verbal methods of communicating consent, but it seems to me that applying the Doctrine of Continuing Consent is closer to the recognition of current law in most jurisdictions (as well as age old conventional wisdom), and is a simple and effective way to conceptualize, describe and to understand the process of seeking step-by-step consent for participation in a sexual act.

Regardless of whether the consent you receive is in the affirmative, continuously, or by carrier pigeon for that matter, <u>having the consent/permission of your sexual partner is absolutely required</u>. And if you are ever accused of or charged with inappropriate sexual behavior—you will be asked (and your jury will want to know) why you didn't clarify what permissions you had, or why you didn't stop when it became unclear what permissions you had.

RECOMMENDATION: I say ALWAYS seek the continuing consent of your sexual partner(s), and NEVER assume you have any kind of consent no matter what consent you may have been given in the past! It is part of being a good lover. You need to be responsive to the needs of your partner, and you need to be aware of what you are doing and how it affects your partner. This is *CRUCIAL* because even if you have one's affirmative consent to engage in a sexual act, it is possible to exceed that level of permission at any time—it is entirely conceivable that you can rape your partner the second time, or by doing something entirely unexpected outside the scope of consent, or by not stopping if consent is withdrawn. Yes, you or your partner can always change your mind about something you've started and withdraw your consent!

THE RULE: *No Forcing or Tricking Anyone To Engage in a Sexual Act,* and you should always seek the Continuing Consent of your partner(s) for all sexual acts, every time.

BEST PRACTICE: As part of the campaign for the "Yes means Yes" legislation in California (SB 967), there was advertising suggesting something to the effect of "Just get a text saying yes." This leads to a whole other level of verifiability and assurances: The demonstrable consent of your partner. If you have such a text, or other demonstrable proof of consent, it is difficult for your partner to claim consent was not given. Again, this means absolutely nothing when consent is exceeded or withdrawn, but it is not a bad idea to seek the demonstrable consent of your partner! It is not only an opportunity to establish permissions, but to also establish boundaries. It might even be an opportunity to communicate expectations, especially with a new sexual partner. (This should become part of every professional athlete's training: "No text, no sex!")

NOTE: If you practice more extreme forms of sexual activity (like BDSM and so forth) where the fantasy doesn't necessarily facilitate lovingly seeking the continuing consent of your partner(s), and consent for the acts is usually derived from the willing participation of the parties, it is a very good idea to establish some sort of communication that is representative of consent, and it should be used often. Once that communication is used, consent is thereby reaffirmed (or withdrawn if the parties prefer to incorporate this with any other safe words or actions in place that allow for real communication within the fantasy). Because whether or not consent is part of your fantasy, your practice, or even your beliefs or your native culture—it is critically important in maintaining the freedom, liberty, and autonomy of the individual. And while it might not be important to you now, it will be when your 'cellie' wants a piece of your juicy booty in the middle of the night!

And that goes for you, too, missy! I am not just talking to the boys, here. The example above could have just as easily been about Susie going down on Bob, or Susie fingering Linda. Rape is an equal opportunity crime.

NO GOING ANYWHERE YOU AREN'T SUPPOSED TO GO

The next few behaviors deal with property—specifically private property. <u>All Traditional Western Common Law rules defend the right to own and enjoy private property</u>.

Private property includes real property (land, homes, farms, and businesses), chattel (the stuff we fill our homes and businesses with, including our belongings, pets, livestock, inventory, etc.), and, of course, money (in all of its forms like cash, stocks, bonds, etc). And, each of us has the right to own and enjoy whatever property we may be able to possess, and we are free individually or collectively to make, buy, sell, trade, and collect as much property as we want—as an economic system, we call this capitalism.

Usually, anytime anyone ever brings up the concept of private property, the discussion quickly turns into a debate about the *Virtues of Capitalism v.* the *Virtues of Socialism*, and people separate into their respective ideological camps based on the way they believe things ought to be. I bring up political economies here because it is important to realize that we live in a capitalistic society, and the law recognizes our rights to own and enjoy private property no matter what our political beliefs may be. Besides, much of the discussion in this area is simply becoming more and more academic over time, as the reality is that over the last quarter century or so, former command economies have given way to the private ownership of the means of production, socialistic economies have implemented market solutions where nearly 3/4's of all nations have their own stock exchanges, and capitalistic economies continue to install and adjust social safety net programs and tax incentives to address issues of poverty and fairness. The truth of the matter is that the world has become one big giant 'mixed economy' to varying degrees.

The rule of _No Going Anywhere You Aren't Supposed To Go_ specifically refers to real property, where the rule is that you may not enter onto the property owned, leased, rented, or otherwise occupied by another without permission or consent (see Behavior 14 about Consent/Permission). If you enter onto the property of another without permission or consent, you will be Trespassing. If you do so with the intent to commit a felony (like theft), you will be committing Burglary.

In this day and age, when boundaries are regularly established and fenced off, locks and other security measures regularly installed, and the abundance of 'No Trespassing' signs everywhere, it is difficult to imagine that anyone doesn't understand that the rule is to not go anywhere you aren't supposed to go. After all, everyone wants their own rights to peace and security to be respected and protected, no matter what their political views on the distribution and ownership of wealth happens to be.

NO TAKING PROPERTY OR KEEPING PROPERTY YOU KNOW BELONGS TO SOMEONE ELSE

Theft is one of the most intricate, highly legislated, and constantly litigated of all legal concepts as ownership of property is commonly disputed. Entire bodies of law exist to define the ownership, exchange, entrustment, and liability associated with private property—whether it be real, tangible, financial, or conceptual property. And, over time, a body of law has developed for each type of property.

The thing to realize is that it doesn't matter if the law is protecting Grandma's TV (tangible property law), her home she keeps it in (real property law), or her retirement and investment accounts that pay the cable bill (banking, financial, and securities law)—the concept is always exactly the same: It's all Grandma's property! And the law protects Grandma's rights to her property, no matter what body of law, statute, code, referendum, Supreme Court or common law case articulates her property rights.

Some stuff in Grandma's house isn't hers, like the shows she watches on her TV, even though she paid the cable bill—the producers or the TV stations own the content they broadcast (copyright and intellectual property law). And Grandma doesn't own the name of the company who made her TV either, even though they put it in big, bold letters right on the front of the TV that is in her living room (trademark law). And, there is even a body of law that governs what happens to Grandma's house and TV when she dies (estate law).

The rule about other people's property is that anytime you steal, take without permission, pilfer, jack, lift, leach, snatch, swipe, yank, copy or use without authorization, somehow claim for your own when it isn't, or profit off of something that belongs to someone else, IT IS SIMPLY NOT ALLOWED—NO MATTER WHAT YOU CALL IT OR HOW YOU DO IT!

NOTE: The way you become wealthy is to save, by spending less than you earn, or to create or buy something for a low price and sell it for a higher price. You then invest your savings or surplus earnings to build wealth. While there very well may be great financial inequality in America, there has always been great financial inequality in America. This is the land of opportunity, not the land of financial equality. The only equality we are guaranteed about wealth is the equal opportunity to acquire it (lawfully, of course).

ALSO NOTE: Remember: *You can't buy happiness!* And, if you can't buy it, you certainly can't steal it!

NO DESTROYING / BURNING OTHER PEOPLE'S PROPERTY

As a logical extension to *No Stealing Property or Keeping Property You Know Belongs To Someone Else*, you cannot take any action that would destroy, burn, or otherwise interfere with other peoples' property! It has essentially the same effect as if you were to take it and keep it for yourself because you are depriving the rightful and lawful owner the right to enjoy their property.

Additionally, there are public safety concerns about arson: Fire cannot be easily and readily controlled—fire will consume everything in its path with an unending appetite and must be extinguished as soon as possible. This is why we give great license to the fire department to do whatever it takes to stop fires—even tear your house down to prevent a fire from spreading. It's a concept in the law that is called 'the Greater Good'.

NO MAKING PLANS WITH ANYONE TO DO ANYTHING UNLAWFUL, NO ASKING ANYONE ELSE TO DO ANYTHING UNLAWFUL, NO ATTEMPTING TO DO ANYTHING UNLAWFUL, AND NO HELPING ANYONE ELSE AFTER THEY DO SOMETHING UNLAWFUL

This area of the law is known as the 'inchoate crimes', or crimes that are somehow incomplete or imperfect because there needs to be an underlying plan for some other unlawful behavior. But make no mistake—the plan itself is unlawful! The rationale is that the law prosecutes the guilty mind, and if you plan, assist, solicit or attempt unlawful behavior, it's a crime!

But further: You can be held liable for other people's crimes when you help them in some way commit a crime. Let me say that again: YOU CAN BE HELD LIABLE FOR OTHER PEOPLE'S CRIMES!!! It's called vicarious liability, and it happens <u>all of the time</u>. Getaway drivers and lookouts are found guilty of the crimes they assist, everyone in the crime ring is found guilty for the crimes committed by the crime ring (even the bookkeeper), and ALL of the felons are guilty for a murder that happens during the commission of a felony in which they participated—EVEN IF THEY WEREN'T THE ONE WHO PULLED THE TRIGGER.

And, it is amazingly easy to get suckered into a criminal enterprise! Even I was once suckered into something way larger than I knew just by trying to help someone out. Luckily, the military police detective and my section leader saw that I was only trying to help a fellow soldier pay his bills and feed his kids when I bought cigarettes for him off my ration card so that he could sell them to his German friend at a profit—after all, the Deutsche Mark to Dollar rate fell by almost 200% the year before I arrived in Germany. Little did I know just how many of my fellow soldiers were also 'helping him out' and that his house was filled with all the latest electronics equipment and his kids were eating steak every night! I was very lucky not to go down with him. I offer my own story only to demonstrate how important it is to know the Rules of Lawful Behavior—because it is very easy to violate the law in a very big way when you might not think it's that big of a deal or might only be trying to help someone out. In my case, I was only trying to help a family get by during hard times! I could have been facing 5-10 years in federal prison for racketeering because I knew the purpose of my actions—to sell the cigarettes for a profit, which I really didn't think was that big of a deal. But because I participated, no matter how small a role I played, I was guilty of racketeering. It helped that I didn't take any profit from the sale of the cigarettes (I actually offered to buy groceries for the family), but again, <u>I was very lucky</u>.

THE LESSON HERE: Don't get involved with other people's bullshit—stay out of it! You will only be helping yourself fuck your own life up. Offer to help out in other ways if you can, but stay away from the bullshit.

NO BREAKING YOUR PROMISES

When we make promises, we make our own law. Let me say that again: WHEN WE MAKE PROMISES, WE MAKE OUR OWN LAW! And the courts will honor the law you make for yourself.

Of course, I'm talking about Contract Law. But when you think of it, we control what happens around us by making the law that governs our daily lives that effects such decisions as to where we live, how we live, what goods and services we buy and sell, and what we ultimately choose to do with our lives. It is very empowering to know that the entire fabric of our society will support and enforce the life I make for myself by enforcing the agreements I make with others and ensuring that others will be required to honor and keep the agreements they make with me.

This means we all need to have a rudimentary understanding of what a contract is, so we don't go around legally obligating ourselves when we didn't mean to or find ourselves in the unfortunate position of being taken advantage of. We should all embrace the power of contracts, teach the power of contracts, and become very comfortable with the negotiation of contracts because more and more of our lives are merely a contractual relationship with one another.

Some Basics:

- A contract is when two or more parties are promising each other an exchange of something (like goods, services, property, ideas, or performances) for something in return, usually money. And, if you break your promise, you will be in 'breach' of the contract, another way of saying you broke your promise. There are, of course, volumes of technicalities in contract law addressing all sorts of details and questions that have been hammered out in the courts for a couple of hundred years, and many standards have been created over time that can be found in the Uniform Commercial Code as well as case law. But this simple description is all you need to understand what a contract is—even if a contract is several hundred pages long outlining a series of promises, terms, and responsibilities of what could be many different parties over a long period of time.

- Contracts can be oral (made with words alone) or in writing.

- A contract is formed when the parties agree to the terms of a deal (usually through a negotiation process of offer and acceptance of the deal), and the deal MUST have some sort of an exchange (called consideration) or it is not enforceable by either party.

- If you make a reasonable offer to someone for something and they accept your offer, you will be legally required to honor your offer. Likewise, if you accept an offer from someone else, you will be legally held to your acceptance of the offer.

- You can revoke an offer you make before someone accepts it if you change your mind, but not after they accept it because that would be breach of contract. And you can never revoke your acceptance of someone's offer because that would also be breach of contract. Timing matters in the negotiation process.

- You have the right to accept an offer that is made to you, but as soon as you give a counter-offer, the other party is no longer legally obligated to their original offer (because a counter-offer is seen in the law as a rejection of the original offer—although you can always ask them later if their original offer still stands).

- If you sign a written contract, you will have to follow the terms of the contract you sign—even if you agreed to something different when you signed the contract. (Daytime TV **Judge Judy** often refers to this as the 'four corners rule', because the four corners of the paper are the boundaries of the agreement.)

- If someone breaks a contract with you and you have damages (like a financial loss of some kind), you have to minimize your damages if you can (called mitigation) because the other party will only be held responsible for damages that couldn't be mitigated.

- You never want to be in the position of trying to undo a contract—it's a lot of hassle. But, there are defenses in contract law that can be asserted to make a contract (or parts of a contract) void or voidable by one of the parties (See Behavior 16 for a partial listing of defenses to contract). If you ever feel like you were taken advantage of because of a contract deal you made, research defenses to contract or seek the advice of an attorney right away because you may have recourse. Contested contracts are never final until the courts say they are!

- The only thing a handshake does in the law is show agreement. Don't let anyone intimidate you because you want to examine, clarify, question, or enforce your understanding of the terms of a contract, even if you shook on it!

- You can always modify a contract with further agreement (although further consideration may be required) and the parties of a contract can always agree to cancel a contract if that is what everyone wants to do.

- And if you make a contract for something that is unlawful or somehow illicit, the courts will not enforce it!

Examples of performance in contracts that everyone needs to know (because daytime court TV is filled with these types of claims):

- If you borrow money and promise to return it, you have to return it! Why does everybody always claim the money was a gift?

- If you hire someone to perform a service (like to paint your house or to DJ a party) for a certain amount of money, and they perform the service, you have to pay them for their performance <u>even if they do a crappy job</u>! You could pay them less than the agreed amount as a settlement to any dispute about the crappy performance, but you still have to pay them. If they don't accept what you pay them, they can always take you to court to have your promise to pay the full amount enforced, but then you get to tell the court all about their crappy performance and why they don't deserve the whole payment.

- If you promise to perform a service for a certain amount of money, you will have to perform the service or you will be in breach of contract—and you will be liable for any damages the other party may have as a result of your breach (like having to hire someone else to do the job you were hired to do). You will be required to return any money you were paid in advance, but the law generally does not require payment until after performance of any job or service.

- You can offer a warranty when you sell something, but you don't have to. Generally, the assumption in the law is that a buyer buys something "as is" and the default position is "let the buyer beware." However, the law demands "good faith and fair dealing," so all descriptions must be true, and goods (especially new or custom made goods) need to be free from defects (unless disclosed) and generally be "fit for ordinary use."

Some Advice:

- Take lessons on negotiation. There are tons of free videos on YouTube about negotiation—you should watch them.

- Always take pictures of everything you do, especially when you move in or out of a rental, complete a job for someone, or have an accident of any kind—even if you left the place clean, did a good job, or think there was no damage because of the accident. <u>Pictures can help you tell a story after the fact.</u>

- Always send written confirmation of your understanding of any agreements you make in a text or an e-mail. That way, there is no doubt about the details of your agreement (especially if you lend money to someone you know). This is something that **Harvey Levin** says all the time on *The People's Court*.

Not every promise you make will become law, and you need to know that, too. I have a kind of funny story about my first lesson in this:

When I was a kid in high school, I went to yearbook camp—sort of like band camp or football camp, but we learned about the art of reporting, photography, layout, and what makes for a good yearbook. (You know it's a true story if I cop to going to yearbook camp!!!) And, like all camps you get paired off with other kids in dorms for overnight housing. Sadly, I don't remember anyone I went to camp with, I was so shy and such a dork that I didn't make any lasting friends that week. Besides, I think I was only going to be a sophomore and almost everyone else was going to be a junior or senior.

The guy I was roomies with, for whatever reason, didn't want to shower every day when everyone else showered—probably shy or whatever. But it was hot that summer in Santa Barbara, and I wanted desperately to change rooms because of the growing funk. In making my case about my suffering to the resident adviser and some of the other guys who were there trying to convince me that it wasn't that bad, I said something to the effect of, "I'll give $50 to anyone who lifts that blanket and sniffs that bed!" To my shock and dismay, one of the cool guys standing there was like, "I'll do it." And then he did it!!! Of course, to a chorus of boys making gross-out noises and laughing like crazy. Did that mean I had to pay him $50? That was a lot of money to me back in the day (still is to blow on something like that!). What was my obligation? Luckily, the cool guy let me off the hook, and we all just laughed it off. But, it scared the hell out of me as I don't think I even had that much money with me!

As it turns out, I would have had the legal defense of capacity (I think I was only 15 years old that summer). I probably also had a good argument against formation, as no one in their right mind would have thought I was seriously negotiating for a good bed smelling—it should have been understood my offer was simply for dramatic effect in support of my case of suffering because of the growing funk. But, I offered, he accepted, *and* he performed! These are the essential elements of a contract. Any argument for non-payment would have had to come from me in the form of a defense to contract, which I was simply unprepared to make.

Of course, now I wish I had the maturity back then to simply ask my roommate to take a shower. Or, better yet, offer to keep guard so he wouldn't be embarrassed in the shower room. Maybe I would have even made a friend that week?

CONTRACTS SUMMARY: When your promises constitute a contract, you may not break your promises. Otherwise, you may find yourself in civil court for breach of contract where the law will require you to keep your promises or compensate the other party for your breach. The basic rule of remedy is that the law will put the non-breaching party in as good a position as if the breach were never to have occurred or allowing the non-breaching party the benefit of their bargain.

Additionally, even if the promises we make do not constitute a contract, keeping your promises is the honorable thing to do—no matter what! So, if you don't intend to keep a promise, don't make it in the first place.

THREE REQUIRED BEHAVIORS

In addition to the aforementioned forbidden behaviors, there are behaviors that have been made required of us, they are as follows:

FIGURE 2. THREE REQUIRED BEHAVIORS

Behavior by Number	Required Behavior	Resulting Criminal Charge or Civil Claim
11	**Follow Instructions From Peace Officers** (A peace officer is anyone sworn by a legislating jurisdiction with powers of arrest. Examples: Police, Sheriff, Ranger, Deputy, Highway Patrol, Harbor Patrol, Air Marshal, Fire Marshal, Constable, Border Patrol, State Trooper, Bailiff, FBI Agent, ATF Agent, ICE Agent, etc.)	Obstruction of Justice / Resisting Arrest / Evasion / Failure to Obey a Lawful Order / Tampering with Evidence / Disorderly Conduct / Breach of the Peace / etc.
12	**Follow Laws You Know to Be True** (Like driving according to the rules of the road found in the vehicle code, or following the rules found in any code of law or regulations.)	A 'ticket' for an infraction (a minor or misdemeanor offense), or arrest for a felony violation (a major offense). Fines and penalties are often well publicized to act as deterrent against the unlawful behavior.
13	**Act Reasonably**	Criminal or Civil Negligence (usually accused or charged as a negligent act)

FOLLOW INSTRUCTIONS FROM PEACE (POLICE) OFFICERS

What you have to keep in mind is that police work is really all about control: Quite simply, in order to provide for the public safety and security, the police arrive at situations that are out of control (or believed to be out of control) and then act to gain control of that situation in the interest of and on the behalf of the people of the jurisdiction. Afterward, they determine if any crime has been committed, make arrests, get people medical help, restore order, clear the area, and then they document what happened. That is what they do.

Once the police become involved in a situation that involves you, IT IS IMPERATIVE THAT YOU FOLLOW POLICE INSTRUCTIONS AND ALLOW THEM TO GAIN CONTROL OF THE SITUATION. Because whether or not you like the police, whether or not you trust the police, or whether or not you believe the police are out to get you—they will always act to gain control of the situation no matter who you are. How many celebrities or politicians are on video uttering the phrase, "Don't you know who I am?"

The penalties for not cooperating with the police are not really the problem, a ticket for Obstruction of Justice with a fine, or maybe even a small amount of jail time can fix that—it is the unintended consequences:

ANDY LOPEZ

Andy Lopez was a 13-year-old boy walking through a vacant lot with a realistic looking replica of an assault rifle on October 22, 2013 in Santa Rosa, California.

It doesn't matter that it was only an airsoft gun (pellets, not bullets), or that he wasn't necessarily doing anything wrong, or that he was only going to play a joke on one of his friends as was reportedly assumed to be what he was doing. What matters is that police suddenly came upon him and ordered him to drop the weapon.

Instead of following the instructions from police, allowing them to gain control of the situation and dropping the weapon when told, Andy apparently tried to show the police that it was only an airsoft gun. Andy was shot 7 times and was pronounced dead at the scene as police took defensive action against a suspect who appeared to pose a threat by raising a weapon.

The point was well made all over the news that in more innocent times (if they ever really existed) this would have never happened, and that Sheriff Andy Taylor (from TV's *The Andy Griffith Show*) knew all the kids in Mayberry, didn't even carry a gun himself, and he never would have assumed that young Andy Lopez would ever be carrying a real assault rifle. But the point was also well made that we now live in the times following the Columbine High School shooting, the Sandy Hook Elementary School shooting, and now the Parkland Shooting (and a whole host of other shootings that seem to keep happening)—where atrocities have been committed by young men. If there ever was such a time when no one would have assumed that gun was real, it no longer exists. It can't.

Whatever your parental methodology or beliefs of discipline may be, kids *must* be taught to follow commands from police. For some reason, people now seem to think the appropriate course of action when dealing with the police is to negotiate, argue, and resist police action until the police understand that they didn't do anything wrong, or that it wasn't *wrong enough* to warrant police action. Kids see this behavior and emulate it.

What happened to Andy Lopez is sad and tragic, and we all grieve for the senseless death of a young life. But if kids learn to follow the instructions from police from this horrible incident, and if parents and schools start to teach kids to follow the instructions from police because of this, then Andy's death will not have been in vain. What it all boils down to is that everyone needs to learn to follow instructions from police.

And to anyone who feels that it is wrong to use Andy's story, or anyone else's story that I'm about to use throughout the rest of this book, I am truly sorry. It is definitely not cool to be made into an example. I am not trying to find fault or participate in a cruel game of blame the victim ... but to learn the painful lessons from this and other tragedies. And there are many.

TAMIR RICE

A little over a year later on November 22, 2014, pretty much the same scenario played out for Tamir Rice, a 12 year old boy who was shot and killed by police in Cleveland, Ohio after police responded to a call where they were notified of a black male who "keeps pulling a gun out of his pants and pointing it at people," according to the narrative offered on Wikipedia.

For the love of God, why do parents and grandparents still purchase toy guns for children to play with? I don't care if that's the kind of toy you played with when you were a kid—the age of playing 'Cowboys and Indians' is long over! FOR FUCK'S SAKE!

Tamir was shot almost immediately by police upon arrival—video showed Tamir moving the (toy) gun at his waist as they drove up shouting at him to show his hands. Tamir died the next day.

OSCAR GRANT

Oscar Grant was a New Year's Eve reveler on his way home to Oakland from a San Francisco fireworks display on January 1, 2009.

Without regard to what led up to Oscar being detained in the early morning hours on the BART platform by police, Oscar was instructed by police to sit down, put his cell phone away, and be quiet (as widely reported and re-created in the film *Fruitvale Station*).

Were the police instructions right? Fair? Just? It doesn't matter. What matters is that Oscar was detained by police and that the instructions were given. We all have equal access to the courts for redress of our grievances after-the-fact if we don't agree with the way we were treated by police. But if you are being detained by police, you must follow their instructions, or you will most likely find yourself being forced to comply with those instructions.

Instead of following police instructions and sitting down, putting his cell phone away, and being quiet, Oscar decided to get up in the middle of a police matter to apparently discuss the situation with them. He then resisted the physical force police used to force him to comply with their instructions. The horror that happened after that has been seen over and over again because bystanders captured the event on cell phone video as Oscar was shot at point-blank range in front of dozens of BART riders. Officer Johannes Mehserle said he pulled his service revolver from his utility belt by mistake instead of his taser. Yes, a lot went wrong in the early morning hours of that new year and deadly mistakes occurred—but mistakes can't happen if the situation which allows for the mistakes doesn't happen in the first place. The entire tragedy could have been avoided if Oscar had simply followed instructions from police.

A NOTE ABOUT SURVIVING POLICE DETENTION: If you are being detained by police, you have somehow given police reasonable suspicion that you might be involved in criminal activity or may have otherwise violated the law. Detention is the first step towards an arrest, where there is a cursory investigation into the facts that gave rise to the suspicion against you—and it could be almost anything that makes you somehow seem suspicious, which could be circumstances way beyond your control and you have no idea about like you match the description of someone else. <u>You need to allow the investigation to occur, and your cooperation during the investigation is only prudent</u>. What you need to realize is that there are really only three basic outcomes which will most likely occur from a police detention: 1) You are let go, 2) You are given a ticket, or 3) You are arrested. Which of the three happens to you depends on the evidence they gather during their investigation regarding your guilt or innocence of a violation of the law, and your attitude toward them during their investigation. If the level of suspicion against you rises to the level of probable cause (meaning that a suspicion against you is supported by circumstances sufficiently strong enough to justify a reasonable belief that certain facts are probably true), you will be subject to even further search and investigation.

SOME NOTES ABOUT COOPERATING WITH THE POLICE: When I say that your cooperation during the investigation is only prudent, I am talking about your general demeanor or the attitude you display. You MUST be polite, civil, and respectful to police, or you will be treated as "combative", "uncooperative", or "non-complying," and will likely face an escalation of force until you comply. When I was in the army, this general demeanor was called "respect." When I was a kid in school, it was called "being on your best behavior." In business it is called "professionalism." <u>The police call it "cooperation."</u> Sadly, the phrase "cooperating with police" has become confused with "being a cooperating witness for the state." Yes, one can become a cooperating witness for the state by providing incriminating information to police/authorities, but that's not what I am talking about when I say your cooperation during the investigation is only prudent—I am only referring to your demeanor during a police encounter. For the best experience with police, you should answer all questions, "Yes, Sir," or "No, Ma'am," make direct eye contact, and be as respectful as you possibly can be.

If Detained by Police, You Should:

- Keep still, and don't make any sudden movements.

- Keep your hands where they can be seen at all times.

- Do exactly what you are told, and ONLY exactly what you are told.

- Don't reach for anything!!! If you are asked for something, like your driver's license, and you don't have it ready to hand to the officer, tell the officer where it is. ("My ID is in my wallet in my back pocket, officer, would you like me to get it for you?") Let the officer direct your every movement—if they want you to reach for it, they will tell you.

- Never be disrespectful—offer no sarcasm or attitude. Tell the officer(s) you intend to fully cooperate and that you will comply with all of their instructions.

- Your tone of voice should be pleasing at all times.

- Never show any aggression or pose any kind of threat to police.

If You Get Pulled-Over:

- A traffic stop is a police detention—follow all the directions outlined above!

- Put your drivers' license and registration in plain sight on the dashboard <u>if you can</u> before the officer approaches your vehicle. If you do not have time, leave them wherever they are. (Keeping documents at the ready is not a bad idea.)

- Turn off the car and radio, put down your snacks and drinks, put out your cigarette, and roll down your window.

- Before the officer approaches your vehicle, put your palms on the steering wheel with your fingers pointing upward and fanned out.

- If you are a passenger, put your hands on your lap with palms up and your fingers pointing outward and fanned out.

- Stay in the car—do not get out of your vehicle unless you are told to do so.

- Follow all directions you are given, and again: DON'T REACH FOR ANYTHING UNLESS YOU ARE TOLD TO DO SO!!!

The above information is CRUCIAL for you to know and understand. Until the police have complete control of the situation by knowing who you are and what's going on, they don't know what kind of threat you might be to them. If you reach for something when you are not told to do so, or you continue to reach for something when you are told to stop, you will likely face an escalation of force.

One tragic example of a failed traffic stop is **Philando Castile**, who was shot in Falcon Heights, Minnesota, on July 6, 2016 when he continued to reach for his wallet after he was told by Officer Jeronimo Yanez to not reach for his weapon. Castile had told Yanez that he had a weapon in his possession. Out of fear for his own safety, Officer Yanez shot Castile 7 times, who's dying moments were live-streamed on Facebook. It was determined that Officer Yanez's fear under the circumstances of Philando's cooperation was unreasonable, and therefore the shooting was not justified. Officer Yanez was tried and acquitted of manslaughter and reckless discharge of a firearm in a tragic conclusion to a horrible, split-second, over-fearful reaction to someone reaching for their wallet. The takeaway: If you don't have your ID already in your hand ready to give to police, tell the officer where it is and wait for his or her instructions—don't just start reaching for stuff in the middle of a police detention! (Please see Section 4 for information on Justified Behaviors, Behavior 13 for information on Reasonableness, and Behavior 16 for information on Self Defense.)

NOTE: There Are Limits to the Amount of Cooperation Required: There are limits in the law to the amount of cooperation you need to provide police that act as a check and balance against abuses of power and corruption. These limits are contained in the United States Bill of Rights, and in the 'Miranda Warning' given at the time someone is arrested.

Essentially, you never have to consent to any search of your person or property (4th Amendment), although the police may have cause and be justified to search your person or your property in certain circumstances; You may remain silent and not answer any questions (5th Amendment), although it has been held that you will need to affirmatively assert a desire to remain silent and not just be silent when questioned; And if you are arrested, you have the right to an attorney even if you cannot afford one (6th Amendment). Generally, these constitutional rights extend to all people in this great country, not just citizens of our country, and your constitutional rights exist whether or not you are placed under arrest.

If someone having an encounter with police wanted to fully protect their constitutional rights:

- They would not give permission or consent for any search of their person or property if asked. If a search occurs, they would not resist in any way, but they would state that they do not consent to the search.

- They would clearly state that they intend to exercise their right to remain silent when questioned, then remain silent other than to give their name or maybe a very brief explanation of what's happened (please see Behavior 15 for more information regarding Making Statements to Police/Authorities).

- They would ask for a lawyer right away if placed under arrest.

(Please see Behavior 14 about Consent/Permission for a discussion about Consent and the Authorities for more information about protecting your constitutional rights.)

A NOTE ABOUT RESISTING UNLAWFUL ARREST: Traditionally, Americans most certainly had the right to resist unlawful arrest, especially on the American Frontier when the West was being settled and deputies were often untrained and used the law in heavy handed ways without regard for legal rights or procedures. In some jurisdictions, the right to resist unlawful arrest still exists today. However, this isn't the Frontier any longer, and most courts will find that an arrest by a uniformed police officer in the course of duty will be considered lawful—even if it is an arrest of the wrong person altogether with false accusations of guilt. And most jurisdictions now prohibit the use of force to resist arrest, even if you believe that you are being unlawfully arrested. If you are ever faced with arrest, the best thing you can do for yourself is to 'go easy' into custody and to not resist. It can all be sorted out at a later time. Again, we all have equal access to the courts for redress of our grievances after-the-fact if we don't agree with the way we were treated by police.

ERIC GARNER

Eric Garner was selling 'loosies' (loose cigarettes from a pack of cigarettes) on the streets of Staten Island, New York, on July 17, 2014.

When undercover police approached him, he told them to "Get away ... Every time you see me, you want to mess with me ... I'm tired of it ... It stops today ... I'm minding my business ... Please just leave me alone." When officers attempted to handcuff him from behind (apparently he was being arrested because he didn't have the required license to sell tobacco products, and for tax evasion since the packs of cigarettes didn't have the required NY tax stamp), Garner swatted their arms away. Officer Daniel Pantaleo then used a chokehold to subdue him, which at the time was an unsanctioned use of force. Garner was pronounced dead an hour later at the hospital after being treated by medics at the scene.

What is important to realize is that the more you resist, the more force will be used against you. The more of a threat you pose, the more force will be used against you. The irony is that with more and more police incidents and altercations coming to light with the advent of social media, the more people feel emboldened to resist, talk back, defy, and disobey police instructions—usually only to discover that they are only met with more and more force against them. Again, police work is all about control—and the police will always act to gain control no matter how much force is necessary.

THE MCKINNEY, TEXAS POOL PARTY

June 5, 2015. Police respond to a disturbance at a neighborhood pool party where there were uninvited guests crashing the party playing loud music with obscene lyrics, along with a physical altercation between a middle-aged woman and a teen-aged girl. Video taken went viral.

You can look at this event through any number of lenses (like the lens of racism or the lens of police brutality), but in the end it is only a video showing police desperately (and badly) trying to gain control of a chaotic scene with a bunch of kids running around not following police instructions. The more the kids wandered around indignantly, the more the police acted to gain control of the situation. The more the kids didn't listen and follow instructions, the more force was used upon them until they complied.

FERGUSON, MISSOURI AND
THE SHOOTING OF MICHAEL BROWN

On August 9, 2014, 18-year-old Michael Brown went to a convenience store and stole (or took without permission) some Cigarillos (a brand of cigar). When he was confronted by the store clerk, he pushed and chased the store clerk out of the way before leaving the store. Police were called and were given a physical description of the robbery suspect. Minutes later, police encountered Michael Brown, who was walking down the street with a friend. After a physical altercation, Michael was shot dead by police in the middle of a busy residential street. Officer Darren Wilson said that Michael had attacked him and charged at him.

There were conflicting eyewitness statements, and several witnesses of the shooting claimed that Michael had surrendered by raising his hands above his head before he was shot by police (although these accounts were later discounted as not credible). This, along with police leaving the body in the street for several hours and what was seen as inherently bad policing and bad community relations, sparked protests and civil unrest that spread to other communities nationwide for many months. "Hands up, don't shoot!" became a central protest theme, and it was printed on banners and tee-shirts.

HANDS UP, DON'T SHOOT IS GOD-DAMNED RIGHT! WHEN SOME-ONE SURRENDERS, THEIR SURRENDER MUST BE RECOGNIZED AND ACCEPTED! The surrender is an ancient, time honored tradition which has been recognized throughout the eons. It is how we communicate to police that we intend to comply with their instructions, and hands-over-your-head is an international signal of surrender.

Sadly, however, a surrender is often used by suspects as a last resort—when they run out of all other options (and anyone who ever has any encounter with the police is always considered a suspect). For a surrender to be effective, it should be offered early in an encounter and offered unconditionally. The only viable way to avoid an escalation of force with police is to surrender.

Officer Wilson was not indicted on any charges after an exhaustive Grand Jury hearing and investigations from multiple government agencies. The DOJ issued a report on March 4, 2015, and Attorney General Eric H. Holder Jr. concluded that "The facts do not support the filing of criminal charges against Officer Darren Wilson in this case."

The civil unrest that followed the shooting of Michael Brown brought into the national spotlight many social issues that (still) exist in America today. The thing to realize with police encounters is that *both* police and suspects alike have a responsibility to deescalate the situation and seek peaceful resolution. That deserves to be repeated: BOTH POLICE AND SUSPECTS ALIKE NEED TO DEESCALATE SITUATIONS AND SEEK PEACEFUL RESOLUTION! The choice before any suspect is to surrender or face an escalation of force. And the choice before any officer of the law is to be the agent of justice they have sworn to be or to become that which they seek to control.

A NOTE ABOUT CIVIL UNREST AND PROTESTING: Throughout American history, we have always sought change through protest. Our history is full of unsavory acts and the rebellion that follows—that has been the American Way ever since the Boston Tea Party in 1773. Through protest, we continue to refine what it means to be American.

Protesting of this generation is no less important than any other. Whether we are demanding equal treatment by police or we are recognizing the failed economic practices of the banks and of the wealthy (the Occupy Movement), protesting is a primary method of communication whereby the people communicate their dissatisfaction.

In my humble opinion:

- We *should* expect and be demanding equal treatment by police. Justice is supposed to be blind (as depicted by the images of Lady Justice, blindfolded, as she is holding the Scales of Justice in one hand and the Sword of Punishment in the other). Police work and law enforcement needs to be objective and impartial while working to embody the principles of justice—blind to race, sex, creed (religion), age, national origin, cultural background, social status, wealth status, sexual orientation, and every kind of disability.

- We *should* expect and be demanding that banks and financial institutions employ and provide sound financial services; and we *should* have demanded that those responsible for the investing practices that led to the housing bubble and financial crisis of 2008 which ultimately led to millions of home foreclosures and wiped out shit loads of savings and retirement accounts <u>face prison time for their irresponsible actions</u>; and we *should* be demanding that the regulations that were put in place to stop that shit from ever happening again (Dodd-Frank) are kept in place!

- We *should* expect and be demanding that our political leaders heed the warnings of science and embrace empirical knowledge as policy is developed about how to address the serious issues facing us today such as climate change, our dying oceans, extinction of whole species of animals, our food supply, disease, and now pandemics among a whole host of other conditions that require serious consideration and analysis.

- We *should* expect and be demanding that our political leaders act to protect and preserve the offices of government they were elected or appointed to hold and not act to undermine the foundations and structure of our representative democracy.

- We *should* expect and be demanding accountability of purveyors of news and demand that news and social media outlets deliver true and reliable information or face penalty when misleading or one-sided news is circulated.

- We *should* be demanding reasonable and affordable health care for everyone in our country.

- We *should* be demanding that women do not have to put up with sexual harassment and are paid equally for equal work.

- And, soon enough, we will probably have to demand restoration of rights already acknowledged by law that some seek to restrict again.

- Etc. etc. etc.

These types of demands become the political discourse of our democratic nation as they represent the will of the people. But blocking traffic, burning police cars, and calling for the willful destruction of property is only counterproductive as the message is lost to violence. Hell, it is difficult enough just trying to communicate a valid political message during a peaceful political protest—just ask **Colin Kaepernick**.

A Note about the Lawfulness of any Instructions from a Peace Officer: There is a lot of debate out there about what kind of instructions police are allowed to give and what constitutes a "lawful order." While it is generally true that one would not be required to follow any *unlawful order* given by police, the only way to determine if any specific order given to you by police is, in fact, unlawful would be to go to court and have it ruled unlawful by a judge. There are many videos on YouTube, and other social media, that show people challenging police and trying to assert their freedoms by resisting police action and adopting resistance techniques for whenever dealing with police. All of that falls into the category of the idea that you could spend a lot of time and energy learning all the boundaries and intricacies of the Rules of Lawful Behavior so you can avoid liability or act without penalty (maybe out of principle, maybe out of some inflated sense of entitlement, or maybe even out of a sense of duty to challenge societal norms), but that is not going to stop police from always acting to gain control of every situation they encounter, nor change the fact that it has been made a requirement to _Follow Instructions from Peace (Police) Officers._

A NOTE ON FILMING THE POLICE: It has been upheld that it is perfectly lawful to film the police. Video is truly awesome because it allows everyone to witness the police encounter for themselves—whether it is from a bystander, a police body cam, or those involved in the police incident. But the filming of a police encounter needs to be entirely incidental to the police encounter.

- If you are a bystander: Your right to film police is guided by _Glik v. Cunniffe,_ a 2011 case before the United States Court of Appeals for the First Circuit where the court cited the "clearly established First Amendment rights in filming the officers in a public space." The Los Angeles Police Department has even published guidelines for filming the police which you can find on their website.

- If you want to film a police encounter that involves you: First of all, I would always try to record any police encounter I have. The problem is that if you are holding a recording device during the encounter, the police can, and probably will, tell you to stop recording as it will most likely obstruct their law enforcement activity. They can also claim that it may be physically used as a weapon against them. At that point, you really have no choice but to follow police instructions and you may lose the opportunity to record the encounter. The best thing to do is to set your recording device in a place where it will record the encounter, but not become part of the encounter.

- If police want to confiscate your recording device: Police generally have no right to seize your property without a warrant. However, if they believe that your recording device may contain evidence of a crime, they most certainly can seize it. You can always preserve your right to film by using a live stream recording service.

FOLLOW LAWS YOU KNOW TO BE TRUE

This should be the easiest rule of Lawful Behavior for anyone to grasp—it's an expression of everything you have ever been taught about what is lawful and what is not lawful. Over time, almost everyone has come to know bits and pieces of the law by being told what to do by your parents, studying in school, watching TV, learning how to drive, going to work each day, and being involved in everyday American life. This is the law you already know to be true, and this book changes none of that. You need to *Follow Laws You Know to Be True*.

But, this is also where the rules of Lawful Behavior start to get a little complicated, too. It seems that advocates from all sides of ideology (religious, liberal, conservative and special interests) have adopted the Nanny State methodology and are using the law and the courts to influence and control more and more of our behavior to the smallest of detail. Legislating and litigating morality has become quite in vogue, legalizing or forbidding all sorts of very personal behaviors, like who we can marry, who can use what bathroom, how large our sodas can be at the local convenience store, the legality of using marijuana, and revisiting old arguments, like abortion rights. Some people are so frustrated that they are ready to just give up on even trying to know or follow the law at all, or they feel they don't have to follow the law because it somehow conflicts with their beliefs or interpretations of legal principles. And, it has become all too common for politicians to use the law and governmental regulations to create 'wedge issues' to 'energize their base' so that they can gain support and power to advance their political agenda. While the process can be sometimes hard to watch, we have no choice but to ride the roller-coaster of what is and what is not legal while all of these questions get sorted out over time. (I happen to like the old Dutch proverb *leven en laten leven!* or *live and let live!* It seems to me a behavior should only be unlawful if it somehow infringes on the rights of others or is against our collective well-being. Otherwise, who gives a shit?)

A NOTE ABOUT OUR COLLECTIVE WELL-BEING: It is the notion of our collective well-being that gives rise to and the legitimacy of government regulation. Sadly, it is all too common that individuals or groups of individuals will act in their best (and usually very short term) interests that are contrary to the interests of our collective well-being. The mechanism in the law that prevents and protects us collectively from this type of behavior is the creation and enforcement of government regulations. Regulation is not the enemy, regulation protects us from the potential harm from the actions of people who would put their personal interests over our collective well-being.

It is also true that with our lives being more and more a mere contractual relationship with one another, that there are also many sub-sets of rules one must adhere to for pretty much every aspect of our daily lives. Specifically, private codes of conduct for school, work, play, and even where we shop and dine as landowners and business owners put in place protections against the unwanted behavior of patrons (although it should be of no surprise that these sub-sets of rules are concerned with exactly the same core set of human behaviors that this book is all about). We must also know and follow these sub-sets of private rules or face some sort of private penalty, like being kicked out of school, getting fired, or being banned from the store or restaurant. It is easy to start to feel the weight of the regulation surrounding us.

And, as icing on the cake, we have over-zealous law enforcement, too: Just look at the death of **Sandra Bland**, whose death in July of 2015 can be directly attributed to the actions of an overly-aggressive police tactic used in Prairie View, Texas: State Trooper Brian Encinia came from out of nowhere and started to follow Sandra so closely that she felt compelled to get out of the police cruiser's way. Only, she failed to signal as she changed lanes to get out of the way, allowing the trooper to pull her over for the violation of failing to signal. Was Sandra racially profiled? Was she picked on as an outsider because of the Illinois license plates on her car? Or was she just a target in the state trooper's window of opportunity? Regardless, the preemptive actions of the police started a chain of events that led to Sandra's death, although this case could have also been an example for Behavior 11, *"Follow Instructions From Peace (Police) Officers,"* because, like a swimmer caught in a riptide, Sandra's only option at that point was to follow the instructions from State Trooper Brian Encinia until she was able to get free.

A NOTE ABOUT CAUSATION: Causation is a complex and multifaceted legal standard that must be established before liability can attach to any criminal or negligent act. While State Trooper Brian Encinia set in motion the events which led to Sandra Bland's death, he certainly wasn't the *cause* of her death. An alleged suicide is not a foreseeable result from the use of an overly-aggressive police tactic used to pull someone over to give them a traffic ticket, and there were certainly intervening events between Encinia's act and the death two days later. And, Encinia's behavior is privileged to the extent he was acting within the scope of his responsibilities as a state trooper. However, one has to wonder just when we will have enough examples of the abuse of police power and the harm that follows to say that harm from police abuse is foreseeable? There is a reason why all of these unsightly cases get settled quickly—new litigation would create new standards for police conduct.

Sadly, the criminal law case books are full of cases where police have overstepped the boundaries of decency, and the courts then defining the limits of law enforcement and the rights of the people from those circumstances. One could argue that the system is working as it always has, but it is all moving so very quickly now with the advent of social media and the 24-hour news cycle! It makes me wonder if we are living in the calm before a storm slowly forming, and I question if we are living in some kind of a golden era of peace and tranquility before some incendiary future event that will end up destroying this social experiment that we call Representative Democracy. Are we in the lead up to that event now?

I'm sure everyone has a story (or knows someone with a story) about a speed trap, some party that got broken up, a bad vehicle tow, some parking meter, or some other crap where someone was singled out unnecessarily by over-zealous law enforcement—it is all too common! Seat belt law enforcement has morphed into just a way to justify pulling someone over who they want to pull over, and prosecuting low level statutes like weed possession seems like only a way to arrest someone they otherwise don't have cause to arrest—like the old-timey prohibition-era gangsters they were only able to imprison for tax-evasion. There is even a term for this: Selective Enforcement/Prosecution. And, there are now news reports that law enforcement is now even being used as revenue generation for municipalities where the outsourcing of the collection process for court imposed fines creates a sort of micro-economy around collections—leaving many people unable to pay their debt to society and get in good standing with the law (Vice News). Just when did the law become a weapon to be used against the people?

It is very easy for me to have a love/hate relationship with law enforcement.

All frustration, anger and fear aside, we all need to follow laws we know to be true:

- Don't commit criminal acts. (See previous behaviors.)

- Follow the rules of the road. (Like no speeding.)

- Know and follow local laws and ordinances. (No fireworks means no fireworks.)

- Read and follow what the posted signs say wherever you are. (Park closes at sunset.)

- Know and follow the rules of your school (like no weapons), and at your workplace and the places you frequent (like no smoking, or whatever).

- Pay your taxes and any fines you incur (like parking tickets) so you stay in good standing with the law.

- Care for your kids, always keep your dog on a leash, and don't litter.

- Etc. Etc. Etc. (It's not that hard!)

And you will want to learn how to behave around police so that you don't look *Reasonably Suspicious* or inadvertently give *Probable Cause* because of your behavior.

If you happen to encounter police:

- Relax. If you look nervous, they will want to know why you look so nervous with the police around.

- Let them give you the stare—ignore them, or simply smile and give a nod back.

- Always wear your seatbelt and make sure your brake lights and turn signals work so you won't get pulled-over for something entirely preventable.

- Never loiter in public areas to avoid looking like you are up to something.

- Always avoid shady situations so that you don't get caught up in other people's shit.

- And most importantly: NEVER, EVER, EVER RUN AWAY—it is almost an admission of some kind of guilt that is most certainly going to be met with an escalation of force.

In this day and age where prisons are privatized and the system actually profits from mass incarceration, this is all of uber critical importance. If you go running around thinking that the system is all wrong and that you have the right to act out—then you will eventually face consequences of your own making. There, you've been warned!

ACT REASONABLY

Let's recap for a minute: Lawful Behavior starts with the recognition that we must understand the limits and boundaries of our individual will in relationship to others and their individual will (Behaviors 1-3) ... that we must respect the life, liberty, and freedom of others (Behaviors 4-5) ... that we need to understand the property rights we all enjoy under the law, (Behaviors 6-8) ... that even a plan for unlawful behavior is unlawful and that it's possible to be held responsible for the behavior of others (Behavior 9) ... that we cannot break our promises when they constitute a contract (Behavior 10) ... and, that we are all required to follow instructions from peace officers and follow all laws we know to be true (Behaviors 11-12). But what happens when someone else's freedom to do whatever their freedom entitles them to do, infringes upon *your* freedom to do whatever your freedom entitles *you* to do? What happens when a list of do's and don'ts isn't sufficient enough to referee our competing interests? And when there are competing interests, what competing interest wins?

Popular culture seems to offer many answers to this fundamental question. Many believe that whoever gets to a place first wins, and they get to make all the decisions and rules. Others believe the most popular, richest, or coolest get to make the decisions because, of course, they should be listened to. It used to be that white men made all the rules in this country. Some believe that the majority should rule, while many insist that what they think is right ought to be what occurs. And, of course, the strongest always think that *they* get to make the rules (See Behavior 1). All of these are wrong. The overarching principle that guides behavior in a free society is reasonableness. And the thing that *ought* to occur is the *most reasonable thing*.

So, what is reasonableness? Simply, as applied to behavior, reasonableness is the objective standard of how a situation is seen through the eyes of a third party. In the law, what is reasonable is not what you personally (subjectively) happen to think is reasonable about how you are behaving, but what somebody else (objectively) would think of your behavior. That somebody else is an unnamed, unidentified person called a reasonably prudent person. And a reasonably prudent person would embody all the principles of the dictionary definition of reasonableness: "Not excessive; being of sound judgment; logical; fair and sensible" or something like that. But that's only half of it.

The other half is the circumstances and timing of any behavior, and how one's behavior relates to the behavior of those around them. For example, it is perfectly reasonable to dance around and shout to your friends across the room at a party, but that behavior is absolutely not reasonable in a quiet library filled with people reading and studying. Reasonable behavior is the appropriate behavior for the circumstances or situation you find yourself in, as seen through the perspective of a reasonably prudent person.

So, for everything you do there can be a judgment of whether or not your behavior was reasonable. The question becomes, "Would a reasonably prudent person say that what you did was not excessive or outrageous, of sound judgment, logical, fair, generally acceptable, and sensible for the circumstances you were in?" If the answer to that question is yes, then it would be said that you acted reasonably at the time of that behavior. If no, then you will have acted unreasonably.

By itself, unreasonable behavior is not unlawful. But, when you behave unreasonably AND you cause harm, injury, or damage to another, that is called Negligence. When you are found to be negligent, you are liable in civil court for the cost of the harm, injury, or damage you cause (when you owe a duty, but, generally, you owe a duty of due care to everyone you could harm). If multiple people are at fault (meaning they also failed to act reasonably and they somehow contributed to the harm, injury, or damage), they will share liability based on their percentage of fault in most US jurisdictions. You can also face criminal prosecution for your negligence if there is a death or serious injury as a result of your unreasonable behavior, or the amount of damages exceeds a certain dollar amount. The reasonableness of your behavior is also important with regard to any interaction you have with the police, whenever a jury evaluates your behavior, and with regard to any justification or mitigation that might apply to your behavior (see Behaviors 17-19 for Justified Behaviors).

What is awkward is that while people used to embrace the idea of being reasonable, and often felt a sense of graciousness in yielding to the rights of others in what was clearly understood as civility, people now just seem to act without regard to the rights of others and compete to win at all cost. Whether it is for a spot on the crowded bus, who gets what lane position while driving, how loud someone talks in the sauna at the gym (my personal pet peeve), or for one of the few flat screen TV's offered at a Black Friday sale—aggressive, inconsiderate and often unreasonable behavior now seems to be the norm.

The irony is that while we have become a culture that generally doesn't care about what other people think of our behavior, our legal system is built upon balancing our competing interests and evaluating our behavior through the concept of reasonableness. The jury system itself is judgment of your behavior, or of claims against you, by usually twelve impartial members of your peers who embody and represent a reasonable perspective. The standard to which you are held oftentimes comes down to what others believe about your behavior considering the application of the law, which become the jury instructions at your trial.

And while you are free to act and behave pretty much however you like, there comes a time when you just need to grow up, grab a pair (tits or balls), and realize that one becomes accountable for their actions through the reasonableness of their behavior—and that the consequences of any unreasonable behavior make it such that to *Act Reasonably* is a behavior that has been made de facto required of us.

A NOTE ABOUT REASONABLENESS AND FREEDOM: Reasonableness is oftentimes the natural limit and boundary of our God-given freedom enshrined in and protected by the Bill of Rights of the United States Constitution. While we have the right to act and speak as we choose without oppression, restraint, or hindrance—we certainly do not have the right to infringe upon the rights of others or place them in any sort of risk of harm or injury. And if you are not acting reasonably, there is a good chance you are infringing upon the rights of others, or there is a good chance you are placing them in some sort of risk of harm or injury.

A NOTE ABOUT REASONABLENESS AND OUR RIGHTS AS AMERICANS: It seems to me that way too much emphasis is placed on our rights as Americans—it only feeds into our culture of entitlement. I believe our rights as Americans are simply the inherent fundamental rights nature or God gave us as living beings on this earth to live our lives according to nature within the constructs of our society. Our government simply acknowledges those basic, inherent rights and articulates this in the 9th Amendment of the Bill of Rights where it states:

> *"The enumeration in the Constitution, of certain rights, shall not be construed to deny or disparage others retained by the people."*

While there are differing views of how to interpret this language, in *Griswold v. Connecticut* (1965), the US Supreme Court found 'emanations and penumbras' from this text, and from other articulated rights we enjoy, to come to a decision in that case that has been the basis for the articulation of several other rights that have since been acknowledged as law.

From a natural law perspective, unless there is a law to prevent your behavior because it somehow infringes on the rights of others, or is against our collective well-being, almost anything you do can be construed as a right retained by the people. While this is a very expansive view of our rights as Americans, it is probably the easiest way to understand our rights. It also shifts the focus from our rights as Americans to our responsibilities as Americans. Because if everything you do is your right to do, then shouldn't you question if you should be doing whatever you are doing in the first place? And doesn't that then make the reasonableness of your behavior the limit of your rights?

Therefore, if you want to know what your rights are in a free country: It is your right to do anything reasonable, not restricted by law. And, if you want to understand your freedom: You are free to exercise your rights, which is to do anything reasonable, not restricted by law.

THREE BEHAVIORS THAT REQUIRE CAUTION

The Rules of Lawful Behavior discussed so far are not really negotiable—they are either forbidden behaviors, or behaviors that have been made required of us. But the next three behaviors deal with situations that are a little more subjective, and if not negotiated well *might* bring you harm. This section offers information that may help you protect yourself in situations that require caution.

And while I would love to believe that all people are intrinsically good and do not act to cause others harm, that civil servants always act in our best interest, and that there are not scam artists out there lurking around every corner for their next victim—well, I would be deceiving myself.

FIGURE 3. THREE BEHAVIORS THAT REQUIRE CAUTION

Behavior by Number	Behavior Requiring Caution	Possible Adverse Result or Crime
14	**Giving Consent / Permission**	You may inadvertently give someone permission to behave toward you in such a way that may otherwise be unlawful, or may not actually be in your best interest.
15	**Making Statements to Police / Authorities**	Perjury (if under oath and your statement is false) / Obstruction (if your statement is misleading) / Inadvertent admission of guilt or fault / Giving a 'false confession' / Waiving your rights
16	**Making Agreements / Signing Your Name to a Document**	You may be held legally responsible for the terms of your agreement or of the document, which leads to the 10th unlawful behavior of Breach of Contract if you break your promises within that agreement.

GIVING CONSENT / PERMISSION

(This is a general discussion about consent. For a discussion specifically regarding consent for participation in a sexual act, please see Behavior 5.)

Consent is like magic—it turns almost any unlawful behavior into lawful behavior. Let me say that again: CONSENT MAGICALLY TURNS ALMOST ANY UN-LAWFUL BEHAVIOR INTO LAWFUL BEHAVIOR! Because American law has traditionally always been about the protection of the individual from the un-lawful acts of others, you generally control the lawfulness of others' behavior against you! Giving your consent to someone for their behavior turns off any pro-tections that the law would have otherwise provided you against that behavior.

This is of uber importance, and it is the reason why I kept referring you to this section throughout this book—pretty much every lawful principle ever stated includes an exception for consent. Almost nothing done to you will ever be con-sidered unlawful if you allow it by consenting to it. In the law, this concept is known as *volenti non fit injuria*, a Latin phrase translated as "to one who is willing, injury is not done." And, once given, your consent is pretty much valid for whatever you consented to until you take it away—it's not like it automatically expires after a certain period of time or anything. That means you must constantly monitor and manage any consent you give! Your consent is so powerful, you can actually give away your constitutionally protected rights!

Your consent is your conscious, voluntary agreement to participate in whatever is happening around you. You can expressly give it (like you say "yes" or you sign a waiver) or you can imply your consent by your actions (like by actively participating). And, you can always assume the risk of injury from another's negligence by knowing, understanding, and voluntarily electing to encounter the risk (like if you were told something wasn't safe but you did it anyway).

Luckily, it is also very easy to revoke your consent: Say no, object to whatever is happening around you, stop participating, leave, or don't do the unsafe thing— but you generally have to act affirmatively to revoke your consent.

Consent is such a big deal that not everyone can freely give it for themselves. One must reach the age of consent before they can give their consent (which may differ from the age of consent for participation in a sexual act—See Behavior 5). I'm talking about the age of consent in its broader sense, where one is old enough to be deemed an adult by reaching the age of majority (age 18 in the United States). By the time one reaches the age of majority (so called because most people in a community are over the specified age), it is assumed that they have acquired all of the knowledge and interpersonal skills necessary to effectively communicate with other members of their community with a strong enough sense of personhood (the quality or condition of being a whole, fully realized, mature, individual person) to adequately protect themselves from the actions of others without parental guidance. It is the age when one's actions become their own, and no one else can answer for them or undo them—signed contracts become valid and one becomes solely responsible for their crimes.

Your consent is something that you should be constantly aware of, and be ready to grant and/or revoke on a moment to moment basis so that others cannot take advantage of you or place you in harm's way.

CONSENT AND THE AUTHORITIES

If authorities (like the police) ever ask you for your consent, you should be prepared to answer that question, too. And it is a big question! Most people probably don't have anything to hide, but you never know what is going on in the mind of the police. Overzealous rule by those in power has plagued mankind throughout the ages, and protections against that kind of thing are in place and enshrined in our Constitution through our Bill of Rights.

A long time ago, I went to a legal job fair, and I got a super cool, bright red, wallet-sized plastic card from The United Way. It states:

> "I do not wish to speak with you or answer your questions based on my 5th Amendment rights under the United States Constitution. I do not give you permission to enter my home based on my 4th Amendment rights under the United States Constitution. I will only permit you to enter my home if you show me a warrant signed by a judge or magistrate. If you have such a warrant, please tell me and then slide it under the door."

I taped it to the inside of my front door and it's been there ever since. I've never had cause to use it, but it's nice to keep there just in case. It's not that I'm trying to hide anything, I'm not. It's not that I'm doing anything unlawful, I'm not. But if the police want to search my home, they need to have a warrant. <u>That is my constitutional right</u>. I don't ever plan to give consent to waive my constitutional rights. The short answer for me to any question like, "May we come in," is always, "Not without a warrant." Additionally, the short answer for me to any question like, "Can I look inside your bag," is also, "Not without a warrant." Politely, of course. The only time I ever consent to the search of my person and belongings is if I want to go into an airport or any other government secured area—then I have no choice but to consent.

I don't have a card for my car, but it would be easy enough to construct:

> "I do not wish to speak with you or answer your questions based on my 5th Amendment rights under the United States Constitution. I do not give you permission to search my vehicle beyond what is visible in plain sight. If you have a warrant to further search my vehicle signed by a judge or magistrate, please provide it to me."

I am not advocating impeding law enforcement by discussing consent and your constitutional rights. It is important, however, for all Americans to know that these protections are in place to help protect your private and personal life against the intrusions of overzealous law enforcement. Trust me, if there is any articulable, reasonable suspicion against you, they will do what's called a "Terry Search" of your person, to make sure you don't have any weapons on you (it's called a Terry Search after *Terry v Ohio, 1968)*. If there is articulable, probable cause against you, they will arrest you and get a warrant to search your home, your car, and your bag anyway.

A WORD OF CAUTION ABOUT OBTAINING THE CONSENT OF OTHERS:
Having obtained the consent or permission for an otherwise unlawful act is a valid and recognized defense to an accusation of unlawful behavior. As a defendant, you will have the opportunity to plead such a defense to a jury of your peers after you have been accused, arrested, arraigned, jailed (or released on bail/own recognizance) until your trial, where you will be able to tell the jury your side of the story after your accuser tells in detail what you did, how you did it, when and where you did it, and hope that the jury believes you over your accuser, in that you in fact had your accuser's consent or permission for any otherwise unlawful act(s) you committed against them. Getting the consent of others for your behavior is not an end-run to following the Rules of Lawful Behavior, and a victim of a crime can never consent to being a victim of a crime.

MAKING STATEMENTS TO POLICE / AUTHORITIES

Another thing police do is interview people. And, they are <u>very good</u> at utilizing multiple interrogation techniques against people as they look for criminal activity and build criminal cases. You will want to exercise caution and be very careful when making statements to the police so that you communicate only what you intend to communicate.

Popular culture and conventional wisdom holds that you don't ever want to talk to the police. And no wonder: Police are notorious for using interrogation and interview techniques that might include lying to you in order to get you to answer their questions (which is perfectly legal to do); saying that the evidence points to you and accuse you of a crime (the Reid Technique); they may try to have a conversation with you in hopes that you might confide in them or somehow slip-up as they gather more and more information about a crime (the HIG Recommendations); they may play roles like 'good-cop/bad-cop' against you; and they may exaggerate circumstances or pretend like whatever happened is no big deal—whatever works under the circumstances to get you to talk so that they can build a criminal case against someone (probably you, since you are the one they are talking to). Invariably, they will tell you a story that is probably pretty close to whatever happened so that you will think they already know everything, but oftentimes they will leave out key points or make it sound like it was somehow your fault so that you will really want to tell them all that you know so they get the whole story—oftentimes under the false pretenses that they are trying to help you.

The thing you need to realize is that a police interview is not the same thing as a trial, and the rules for a police interview DO NOT FOLLOW THE SAME RULES AS A COURT OF LAW. There is no judge who monitors the questions asked of you, and anything you say can and will be used against you!

So, it really can be quite a predicament: On one hand, if you don't cooperate and speak with police or authorities, it will just make you look somehow guilty of something. On the other hand, if you do cooperate, you run the risk that they will use interrogation techniques against you sometimes for hours on end, find inconsistencies, and make new witnesses against you (because the police and investigators who interview you BECOME WITNESSES AGAINST YOU).

BUT THERE ARE TIMES IN WHICH IT BECOMES NECESSARY TO TALK TO THE POLICE AND OTHER AUTHORITIES. Whether you are making a statement to the police as a witness to a crime, become the victim of a crime yourself, have been pulled-over for a traffic offense, have been detained by police for questioning, or someone calls the police on you (weirdly, popular culture seems to have embraced the idea of calling the police for non-emergency situations for help in settling everyday disagreements and disputes, and now there is even a crazy joke or super mean form of personal retribution known as "swatting," where police are called to another person's address for shits and giggles). Arguably, these times require you to communicate effectively with police or other authorities.

While there is a lot of material out there and many books on how to approach other types of communications and interviews (like for a speech or a job interview), there is much less information on how to approach a discussion with police or a police interview. It is easy enough to tell someone to just tell the truth, but no one really tells you *how to tell the truth*—especially in the face of interrogation techniques designed to confuse, lead, and generally trip people up in ways that are not even allowed in a court of law. The question becomes, "How can you communicate a complex set of circumstances honestly and truthfully without getting all tripped up?"

One way to communicate a complex set of circumstances is to take a moment to gather yourself, and then dice up the time period in question into a few very small, true sentences (as few as you can), like this:

1. I wanted to do some shopping, and I got to the store at about noon.

2. I got a cart, and then I went to the fruit section to pick out some peaches.

3. The next thing I knew, some lady was freaking out.

4. I turned around and saw my old housemate, Thomas, staggering toward me.

5. He fell to the floor, and I went to help him.

6. He gasped for air, coughed blood all over me, and then he passed out.

7. Then, the security guard tackled me.

These small true statements become "your truths." Whether you make a formal written statement or you say your truths in an oral interview, the format shouldn't matter because they are your truths.

To someone finding me in this hypothetical predicament, I probably look pretty damn guilty of something! I'm seen with the victim, I'm covered in the victim's blood, I knew the victim, and the security guard thought I did something wrong. But I didn't do anything wrong! I am just a witness! Why would I not talk to police and demand a lawyer when I'm just a witness? I need to be able to give a statement and tell police what just happened! If I freak out, they will probably arrest me for killing him. And at this point, I don't even know what happened. All I know is that he's dead because they just covered him up with a sheet.

Look at my truths above:

- Notice that everything is an 'I-statement' or from the first-person point of view. This is because you can only speak for yourself. Do not try to speak for others.

- Notice that the events are in chronological order. Don't let anyone confuse you. Keep everything in chronological order. If anyone interrupts you, simply start over again. Don't be afraid to repeat yourself.

- Notice that there is no extra information, like maybe at first I thought Thomas was probably just drunk again. If they have questions, they will ask. If the questions they ask are accusatory, simply say "that's not what I said," and repeat your truth. If they ask complex or confusing questions, ask them to repeat the question until they ask a straightforward question you can answer. Answer all questions in full statements, like, "Yes, I sometimes shop here." And if you don't know the answer to any question, simply say that you don't know—but whatever you do DO NOT GUESS!

- Notice that I didn't speculate about anything that happened. If you speculate, it suggests that you might know something more than you are saying. Also, don't repeat anything you are told by anyone else— IT'S A TRAP! If you repeat information you are told about what happened, you are demonstrating that you know something more than you possibly can. Unscrupulous investigators have even been known to purposely feed suspects information to intentionally trip them up during investigations.

- Notice that I didn't say that I didn't kill him or that I didn't do anything wrong. Denying a crime without being asked might make it look like you are lying or have something to hide, and they will inevitably ask you why you would deny a crime when you don't even know what happened?

- Don't get frustrated. Stay calm, and simply repeat your truths. And repeat your truths to whomever asks. They will probably try to switch out investigators to try to catch you in some inconsistency.

- Whatever you do, do not change your truths (your story) because you think that they don't believe you or you think that they want to hear something else. Just expect that they will act like they don't believe you. Just keep saying your truths over and over again, stating answers to questions you've answered exactly the same way you did the first time. Don't let anyone confuse you with subtle nuances or subtle differences to clarify your truths—your truth is your truth.

- Expect long periods of silence. It is a technique of passive aggression that they know drives people crazy. Oftentimes, people can't handle the silence and they just start talking, saying anything that comes to mind. Don't do that.

- Expect that they will ask questions.

- There will come a point where the line will become blurry: Are you giving a statement or are you being interviewed/interrogated? <u>You will need to make a decision if you want to give your consent to their questioning or invoke your constitutional rights.</u>

- Know that it is perfectly okay to invoke your constitutional rights at any time by simply saying that you don't want to answer any more questions and will remain silent moving forward. If arrested, you have the right to an attorney and should ask for one to be present for any further questioning.

- Know that just because they haven't asked you any more questions, anything you still say can and will be held against you.

PLEASE NOTE: This is only a methodology for communicating a complex set of events simply, honestly, and truthfully. It is offered to help you communicate effectively with police and/or authorities.

Continuing on with the hypothetical example above: At some point, I would say to them, "Look, you apparently think I am more involved in all of this somehow when I was only going to do some shopping. Please let me go, or please get me an attorney." Then, I would ask, "Am I free to leave?" I would then not answer any more questions than I already had or offer any further information. I would simply say, "I've told you all that I know. Please let me go, or please get me an attorney. Am I free to leave?"

But don't worry, the police investigation of the hypothetical situation above will consist of all kinds of evidence: My statement, the lady's statement, the security guard's statement, the body, any cameras or other eyewitnesses, any physical evidence found at the scene, and any supplemental information police discover after-the-fact. And if there is enough evidence to suggest that I killed Thomas (if he was, in fact, killed—remember, all I really know is that he died in the store that day), I will be charged with the murder of Thomas and the jurisdiction will have to prove beyond a reasonable doubt to a jury of my peers that I did it (or to convince a jury to say that they believe with like 95% certainty that I did it. If the jury thinks there is only a 50/50 chance that I may have done it, that is not good enough—it has to be "beyond a reasonable doubt").

There are other times in life you might have to make a statement where you would want to exercise caution, too. Most notable would be to a social worker, a hospital administrator, a school administrator, or your Human Resources department. You never know when tragedy may strike, or how close it might strike to you.

NOTE: I should probably add here that I am not a licensed attorney, and I am not giving anyone any specific legal advice regarding how or what they should communicate to authorities about any specific situation. If you are accused of a crime, you should get an attorney. It is the idea that any liability could ever be imputed to me for outlining a methodology of communication that keeps lawyers employed. In fact, let me just give a general disclaimer here: The information provided in this book is for educational purposes, to help you understand the basics of American law and basic legal principles. This book is not meant to provide any legal advice. Should you need any legal advice, you should consult a licensed attorney. I disclaim any liability in connection with the use of any of the information contained in this book. I'm adding this disclaimer because I'm sure someone somewhere is going to have some issue with something I've said in this book and try to blame me for some crazy thing.

MAKING AGREEMENTS / SIGNING YOUR NAME TO A DOCUMENT

This behavior circles back to Behavior 10. It stands to reason that if the law will uphold your legally binding promises, that you will want to exercise caution when making promises or entering into a contractual relationship. (Please see Behavior 10 for a definition of what a contract is, and some basics regarding contract law.)

But even the best negotiators can sometimes get out negotiated, so you will want to know some rules about negotiating a contract. The easiest way to understand some of the rules of negotiating a contract is to look at the defenses to contract:

- **Defense of Duress:** When you are presented with the opportunity to enter into a contract, understand that you are completely free to enter into the contract, or completely free to *not* enter into the contract. You cannot be forced into making a contract—either you agree or you don't. Just know that the other party is also equally free, and they don't have to contract with you either (unless it's with a business open to the public where they will have interstate commerce obligations and be required to treat all contracts with customers the same).

- **Defense of Mistake:** The parties making a contract need to 'have a meeting of the minds' about the subject matter of a contract. This means that all the parties have to be talking about the same thing—one party can't be negotiating for one thing while the other party is negotiating for something different. You can't be in agreement if you are talking about different things.

- **Defense of Unconscionability:** One party cannot have undue bargaining power so as to make the contract oppressive. This is so one party can't make the terms of a contract only beneficial for them. It's kind of like duress, but it's about the forcing the terms of a contract to be one-sided.

- **Defense of Fraud:** A contract will never be upheld if it can be shown to be the means of committing fraud—and many types of contracts are required to be in writing for just that reason (known as the Statute of Frauds).

Sometimes you can negotiate the terms of a contract, others, not so much. Most service providers today now just have a contract that you have to sign (just think of your cell phone provider or your apartment complex). But even if you can't negotiate the specific terms of a contract, you can usually negotiate for more time to consider entering into the contract. If you are reluctant and the other party wants to close the deal, they may offer incentives. If there is ever an agreement to deviate from a standard contract, make sure all parties sign each instance of any changes on the contract AND KEEP A COPY.

If you ever find yourself suddenly in unexpected negotiations you are not prepared for, simply state that you do not intend to enter into a contract without being able to think about it. If an arrangement is truly mutually beneficial, it probably won't have to be made on a moment's notice with lots of pressure. This can get tricky, especially if you want something and there is some sort of competition involved, or there is only a limited opportunity for whatever it is you want. Just keep in mind that when it gets tricky is probably the time when you are most likely to get hustled. It's okay to say you are interested in an offer, and then qualify your interest with the reality of "but only if we can reach an agreement."

Some red flags to watch out for:

- Does the paper you are being asked to sign reflect exactly what is being said?

- Does the paper look right (grammatically correct, no misspellings, etc.)

- Are you the only one signing the paper?

- Does the paper outline steep penalties if you do not do exactly what it says?

- Does the paper require specific settlement requirements in the event of a dispute, like alternative resolution, mediation, arbitration, or evaluation by some group you've never heard of?

- Have you been told that you don't have any choice but to sign the paper?

- Are you being told that you cannot take the paper with you so you can read and sign it later?

- Does it use a lot of language that is hard to understand, or is it written in plain English?

- Have you even read what the paper says?

The only time you ever want to enter into an agreement or sign a contract is after you fully understand all of the terms of a contract, and you agree to all of its terms.

NOTE ABOUT SIGNING A CITATION OR TICKET ISSUED BY POLICE: I include this here, because it is about signing a document, even though by subject matter it should probably go elsewhere, like Behavior 11: *Follow Instructions from Police Officers*. This is AN EXCEPTION to wanting to be cautious—you must sign any ticket issued to you by police. A ticket is not an admission of guilt to any infraction, but a promise to appear before the courts to settle the matter at a later time. If you do not sign, you will face an escalation of force where you will be probably arrested. You will still face the same original charges, only you will face additional charges for not signing the ticket, probably for Obstruction of Justice. This definitely falls into the category of making life much harder for yourself if you fail to comply—even if being given the citation pisses you off so much that you can't breathe! Do yourself a huge favor and: Just. Sign. The ticket. And leave that situation with the satisfaction you do so with your freedom and liberty still intact. The police are not the final arbitrators of any dispute you may have with the state or the criminal justice system—that is the roll of the judge/jury.

My advice to anyone facing any penalty in our mass system of justice is to settle the matter you have with the courts as quickly as you can. If you can avoid appearing before the court by paying the ticket or by going to traffic school to avoid points against your driver's license, then do it! You don't want to be in the situation of having any outstanding or unresolved issues with the courts—it will hinder your future communication with police and your access to the justice system if left unresolved.

THREE JUSTIFIED BEHAVIORS FOR OTHERWISE UNLAWFUL BEHAVIOR

Because American law was founded upon the principles of natural law, there are some behaviors that are considered to be so innate to the human condition that no one can take them away from us. The law recognizes these certain behaviors as reasonable and acceptable, and under very specific circumstances, these behaviors are excused when they otherwise would be considered unlawful—we call these Justified/Privileged Behaviors:

FIGURE 4. THREE JUSTIFIED BEHAVIORS FOR OTHERWISE UNLAWFUL BEHAVIOR

Behavior by Number	Justified or Privileged Behavior	Possible Adverse Result
17	**Self Defense**	Misuse of this privilege will result in your actions not being considered justified, and you will be liable for any unlawful behavior.
18	**Defense of Others**	Misuse of this privilege will result in your actions not being considered justified, and you will be liable for any unlawful behavior.
19	**Defense of Property**	Misuse of this privilege will result in your actions not being considered justified, and you will be liable for any unlawful behavior.

SELF DEFENSE

The principle of Self Defense is that you may use force to protect yourself from physical attack without prosecution or the liability that would normally arise out of using force against another. If you are being attacked, it is normal human behavior for you to protect yourself—and the law recognizes that! The force used to protect yourself or to escape from physical attack is considered to be lawfully justified (having legitimate reason), and privileged (granted with immunity) behavior.

And that's it. Nothing else. That is all there is to the principle of Self Defense. The principle of Self Defense is actually a <u>very narrow permission</u> to use force against another.

The problem is that people are constantly trying to justify their unlawful behavior in the name of Self Defense when it wasn't Self Defense at all.

This is because:

- It is not Self Defense if you hit first. (There is an exception to hitting first, but only when you are attacking your attacker who is threatening you with bodily harm, and you reasonably believe that you are in danger—meaning a reasonably prudent person would also believe that you are in danger, and you absolutely and positively need to use force to protect yourself (see Behavior 13 for a discussion on Reasonableness). This is because you don't need to wait until you are injured by an attacker to be able to defend yourself from an attack).

- It is not Self Defense if you choose to hit back in retaliation. (Because that's a fight! See below for a discussion about fighting.)

- It is not Self Defense if you use force to win an argument, or to somehow assert your will over another.

- It is only Self Defense if you are protecting yourself from (1) an unprovoked attack, (2) which threatens imminent injury or death, and (3) you use an objectively reasonable degree of force in response to (4) an objectively reasonable fear of injury or death.

Self Defense means that you are using force to stop someone from using force against you, and your right to Self Defense ends once the immediate threat from the other party ends. You can only keep using force lawfully as long as force is being used against you, and you need to keep using force to protect yourself or to get away from the attack. It is entirely possible to exceed the privilege of Self Defense and then be liable for any force used in excess of the privilege.

And even if you are acting in Self Defense, you are not privileged to use any level of force you want in order to stop the attack—the force you use has to be reasonable and proportionate in order for it to be considered Self Defense. <u>You may only use deadly force when responding to deadly force</u> (or force that could create death or serious injury). If you respond with more force than is necessary, you will probably lose the right to Self Defense and then be liable for the force you use.

In some jurisdictions, you also have the obligation to retreat from an attack if you can before you are privileged to use force to protect yourself. The easiest way to think about this rule is to imagine that your attacker is a mean, drooling dog with rabies: If you could outmaneuver or avoid a mean drooling dog that was attacking you (or about to attack you) by going indoors, running away, or otherwise retreating—the law says you have to before you are privileged to use force to stop that attack. And that makes sense, why would anyone want to engage a mean drooling dog with rabies and use force to stop it from attacking them if they could just retreat? <u>This is known as the Retreat Rule.</u>

A NOTE ABOUT FIGHTING: Of the myriad of reasons people have for engaging in a physical altercation, Self Defense only applies when defending yourself from attack. While you may very well have to use physical force to protect yourself from attack, if you choose to "take your turn" "swinging back" "hitting" someone who has struck you to engage in a physical altercation—that's called a fight! <u>You simply cannot justify your behavior just because you have chosen to engage in a fight</u>. By choosing to participate in a fight, you are not defending yourself from attack, you are participating in a physical altercation. A very simple test to determine if any force used could be considered Self Defense is to consider whether or not there was a choice to use that force: If someone has a choice to use force—it's probably not Self Defense.

When I was a small boy fighting in the school yard, I was often asked, "Who started this?" And, it was often my defense to breaking the rule of no fighting with, "He started it!" While it was important at the time to learn that the aggressor (the one who hit, touched, or made physical contact first) usually got in more trouble than anyone else who was fighting, <u>it was even more important to learn that the defense of not being the aggressor never worked</u>—we all got sent to the office, and usually home for the rest of the day for fighting. What people don't realize is that when the police ask who started a brawl, it isn't to assign blame—but it is to get to the bottom of what happened. The question "who started it" is a very effective investigation tool that we seem to have been trained to respond to from a very early age. What this all translates to is the aggressor is usually subject to assault charges, and everyone else who participated is charged with disturbing the peace.

A Word of Caution About Self Defense: While the principle of Self Defense is a universally valid and recognized defense in the law today, it is a defense. <u>That means it is considered after it is established that you used force against someone, and the question becomes 'was it a legal use of force?'</u> As with any defense, (also discussed with Consent in Behavior 14,) you will have the opportunity to plead your defense to a jury of your peers after you have been accused, arrested, arraigned, jailed (or released on bail or your own recognizance) until your trial, where you will be able to tell the jury your side of the story and hope the jury believes that you were acting in Self Defense against an attack, which would justify your otherwise unlawful behavior. That is an awful lot of hassle that will have to be sorted out just because you used force against someone—not to mention the pain and expense from any physical injuries you sustain or cause. One might try to avoid such hassle if they could, and only use force as a last resort and as little force as possible.

Looking at Self Defense Options: Whenever you are faced with the threat of an attack, you have three basic options: 1) Avoid the threat beforehand (if you have knowledge of the threat); 2) Retreat from the threat in the moment; or 3) Act defensively to stop or escape an attack. Any other action(s) will most likely not be considered Self Defense.

There are several high-profile cases that have made the headlines in recent years involving the justified/privileged behavior of Self Defense that further illustrate this:

TRAYVON MARTIN

Trayvon Martin was a 17-year-old visiting with family in Sanford, Florida in February 2012, when, on his way home from a convenience store, he was confronted by local neighborhood watch program coordinator, George Zimmerman.

There is no question that there is a whole host of circumstantial evidence that George Zimmerman targeted Trayvon Martin out of racial motivation. There is no question that Zimmerman (by his own admission) acted out of his own unsubstantiated belief and false accusations of some kind of wrongdoing by Trayvon. There is no question that Zimmerman overstepped his authority in his role as neighborhood watch program coordinator when he pursued Trayvon that day through the Florida neighborhood. Trayvon was being targeted and harassed by Zimmerman, and unquestionably, Trayvon had a right to protect himself from Zimmerman's harassment.

At that point, Trayvon really didn't have the opportunity to avoid the threat against him, he was already in the middle of a threatening situation before he became aware of it. It would appear that Trayvon tried to retreat from the threat— he actually lost Zimmerman and hid in some bushes for a time. Regarding his defensive acts, Trayvon had several choices: He had a phone with him and he could have used it to call for help because some crazy guy with a gun was following him; he could have started knocking on the doors of the neighbors to ask for help; he could have tried to make his way back to the convenience store; or he could have had his girlfriend with whom he was on the phone with try to get him some help. He also could have tried to stay hidden out of site from Zimmerman in hopes that Zimmerman would just go away, or he could have tried asking Zimmerman what the hell he wanted and demanded that he leave him alone.

But what Trayvon did, according to Zimmerman and believed by the jury, was to attack Zimmerman and proceed to give him the beating of his life, slamming his head into the cement repeatedly, ironically giving Zimmerman cause to protect himself from Trayvon's attack (known in the law as role-reversal). While Trayvon was entitled to act in his own self defense against Zimmerman's harassment, he exceeded that privilege. Zimmerman then shot and killed Trayvon in what the jury deemed to be justified behavior without regard for who was at fault for the overall encounter. Even if Trayvon had survived Zimmerman's shot, he probably would have been liable for Zimmerman's injuries because he exceeded his self-defensive rights by using more force than was necessary to stop Zimmerman's harassment (unless Trayvon could show that he reasonably believed that his life was in danger, that Zimmerman's harassment was an attack against him, that his actions were necessary for his own protection, <u>and a jury of his peers believed his actions were reasonably necessary</u>).

Trayvon should not have died that day. But this tragedy provides each of us the opportunity to reflect, *"What would we have done"* in that situation—or in any situation where we suddenly find ourselves in harm's way. Sadly, in this day and age, we all need to be mindful of what we are going to do if and when we suddenly find ourselves in a threatening situation.

NOTE: During the lead up to the televised trial, there was a lot of hoopla made over Florida's 'Stand Your Ground' rule. I really wish television correspondents and their guests could get their shit together and actually understand the concepts that they are reporting on and adopt more of an educational role in our society—because by the end of all that hoopla, everyone seemed to have an opinion of the codification of that rule without understanding that <u>the only thing that rule does is remove the retreat requirement</u> from a jurisdiction that once required it, or clarify the law that retreat is not required for an assertion of Self Defense in that jurisdiction.

<u>But retreat is always an option</u>. Shouldn't you at least consider all of your options before acting, especially with the use of deadly force? And if you are on trial for the murder of someone and your claim is Self Defense, you will be asked the question of "Why didn't you just avoid or leave the situation?" And if your answer is a stupid one, like "Because I shouldn't have to," then that should be taken into consideration by a jury of your peers as to whether or not your use of force was really Self Defense when they decide to let you go free or send your ass to prison for 20+ years. In the end, Florida's Stand Your Ground rule wasn't even at issue in this case, and only proved to be fodder for political agendas espoused on the evening news.

THE RAY RICE ELEVATOR INCIDENT

In February, 2014, at the Revel Hotel and Casino in Atlanta, Georgia, football player Ray Rice was seen on video tape striking his then fiancé, Janay Palmer, causing her to become unconscious in an elevator, and then later dragging her out into a hallway.

This is another example of exceeding the privilege of Self Defense. The video footage shows Janay was sort of coming at him in the elevator after they had already been fighting beforehand. It doesn't matter if you know the person who is coming at you, if you are in a relationship with that person, related to them, or they are a complete stranger—if you need to protect yourself from the person who is coming at you, you are entitled to the privilege of Self Defense. But Rice clearly exceeded that privilege by using way more force than was necessary, and his actions were not considered to be justified at all. Rice was arrested for assault (or in this case domestic violence charges were pursued, showing that the violation could have any number of names given by a legislative body).

Looking at Rice's self defense options, Rice probably should not have even entered the elevator with his fiancé to begin with in order to avoid further confrontation. But once he had, he certainly couldn't retreat because he was trapped in the elevator. At that point, his options were to have maybe raised his hands to block her from coming further toward him, tell her to stop, maybe push her away if he was afraid she was going to harm him, or maybe hold her to stop her from any violent behavior she might have engaged in, as those options kind of seem reasonable to me. Anything over that, like striking her so hard as to knock her out, clearly exceeds his privilege to protect himself.

THE SHOOTING OF WALTER SCOTT

Walter Scott was pulled-over by police on April 4th, 2015 in North Charleston, South Carolina for non-functioning brake lights, and was subsequently shot in the back while running away from police. Officer Micheal Slager claimed Self Defense because Scott had grabbed his stun gun.

While Slager's trial for the murder of Scott ended as a mistrial with a hung/deadlocked jury unable to reach the unanimous decision required for the charge of murder, the state of South Carolina was set to retry the case until there was a plea bargain reached settling both federal and state charges.

This is an example of the expiration of the right of Self Defense. There is no question that Slager had the privilege of Self Defense at the moment Scott tried to disarm him, but that specific struggle ended when Scott ran away, ending Slager's right to Self Defense. Slager was not in any imminent danger or substantial risk of death or serious injury when he shot Walter Scott in the back.

The shocking video footage of the shooting that went viral sort of cuts into the middle of the whole event, but still kind of shows in the very beginning what Officer Slager claims, that Scott and Slager struggled over Slager's stun gun. The video then shows Scott running away from Slager, and Slager shooting Scott in the back. This is a case where video evidence incriminates the actions of a police officer, and the reason why police should be required to wear body cameras. And many officers have reported that they welcome the use of body cameras as they also offer proof and protection as to why they made the decisions they made and took the actions they took.

Micheal Slager is now serving a 20-year prison sentence for the murder of Walter Scott.

A NOTE ON SHOOTING A FLEEING SUSPECT: The law allows police to use deadly force on a fleeing suspect when the suspect poses a significant threat of death or serious physical injury to others. Otherwise, dangerous criminals might get away. There was no real evidence that Walter Scott posed any significant threat of death or serious physical injury to others.

A NOTE ON DEADLY FORCE AND THE POLICE: There is only one threshold in the law where the use of deadly force is justified—and that is when one is confronted with deadly force. If you place an officer in a position of being seriously injured or killed (meaning you use deadly force against a police officer), you will have <u>authorized the use of deadly force against you.</u>

In response to recent public outcry, police forces across the nation are implementing "less-lethal" weapons and tactics to subdue suspects. Among these are the use of taser guns, bean-bag rifles, and giving a suspect space and time when possible. It's the "when possible" qualification that makes the use of less lethal force very subjective and up to the judgment of law enforcement involved in any incident. It's policy and a tactic, <u>not the law.</u> The law is that deadly force is justified when one is presented with deadly force. While less-lethal tactics are clearly preferred, police are generally not required to use the least amount of force necessary in performing their duty, but rather it is your responsibility to make sure police understand that you are not a threat.

To show police that you are not a threat:

- Freeze in place!

- Put your hands up! Keep your hands where they can be seen at all times.

- The assumption will be that you are armed until they verify that you are not.

- Drop whatever is in your hands immediately so that whatever it is cannot be mistaken as a weapon.

- Follow all commands and do exactly what you are told.

- And again—never reach for anything during a police encounter unless told specifically to do so (please refer to Behavior 11 for more information on surviving a police detention).

It is also important to understand that the use of deadly force against a suspect is not predicated or based upon a suspect being armed. Many things can be considered a deadly weapon (like a knife, a rock, or even a car), and there are many ways to inflict serious injury that would give rise to the use of deadly force. Even the appearance that you might be armed can qualify the use of deadly force against you—just look at **Stephon Clark**, who only had a cell phone in his hand when police shot him in his grandmother's back yard on March 18, 2018 in Sacramento, California. The problem is that police didn't know if they were about to be attacked in that split second at seeing something in Stephon's hands. Criminal charges were not filed against the police officers.

NOTABLE OMISSIONS: There are many cases of note related to Self Defense and use of force that are not included in this book. Most notable are the cases of **Laquan McDonald** and **Mario Woods**. While there are lessons to be learned from these and other cases of note (especially the distinction between a situation and an attack within a situation), it is not the intent of this book to offer comment on all related cases—but to extrapolate the Rules of Lawful Behavior from cases that lend themselves to do so.

NOTE ABOUT THINKING THAT SELF DEFENSE IS YOUR RIGHT: The privileged behavior of Self Defense is often described as a right enjoyed by Americans. While this may be true, it is not specifically articulated in the US Constitution or the Bill of Rights, and would therefore be considered a right "retained by the people" as articulated in the 9th Amendment of the Bill of Rights. (Please see Behavior 13 for a discussion on our Rights as Americans.)

DEFENSE OF OTHERS

The principle of Defense of Others is exactly the same as Self Defense as applied to defending others. If you see someone being attacked, you may act to defend them as you would yourself without prosecution or the liability that would normally arise from using force against someone. If you see someone who is being attacked, it is normal human behavior for you to want to help them—and the law recognizes that, too! The force used to protect someone else from physical attack is considered to be lawfully justified behavior.

BE CAREFUL: It is hard to tell just who the victim is sometimes. Some jurisdictions even restrict the Defense of Others to be only valid when the person you defend can qualify to use Self Defense for themselves. How would you feel if you happen upon a scene where an undercover cop is trying to arrest a dirt-bag child molester and you ended up helping the child molester get away? And how would it feel going to jail for it?

What I find to be a disturbing trend is that a lot of people just stay on the sidelines now and video violence as it occurs around them. Not to say the video isn't helpful as it shows us all what happened—but *really*? Is that the full extent of your helping out someone in need? How about trying to stop the attack, getting help, or calling the police?

DEFENSE OF PROPERTY

The principle of Defense of Property is a little different from Self Defense or Defense of Others in that IT IS NEVER JUSTIFIED TO USE DEADLY FORCE TO PROTECT YOUR PROPERTY! Otherwise, if someone is taking your property you may use non-deadly force to protect your property without prosecution or liability that would normally arise from using force against someone. If someone is messing with your stuff, it is normal human behavior for you to protect your stuff—and the law recognizes that, too! The non-deadly force used to protect your property is considered to be lawfully justified behavior. But, it's only stuff! Your stuff is replaceable and not worth going to the hospital over or dying for!

SOME NOTES ON DEFENSE OF YOUR HOME: Generally speaking, there are no special protections in the law that allow you to protect your home. In the majority of US Jurisdictions, your home is simply considered your property.

HOWEVER, there are some generalizations you can make:

- If you are home and your home is invaded, your defensive behavior will generally be considered Self Defense, not Defense of Property. Again, you may use reasonable and proportionate force to protect yourself from an attack. And, you never have to retreat from your own home when protecting yourself (known as the Castle Doctrine).

- If the attackers have weapons or threaten you with serious injury, that would be considered deadly force—and you can always use deadly force to protect yourself when responding to deadly force. Some jurisdictions allow the use of deadly force in your home at all times.

Be careful not to use excessive force against someone <u>who is outside</u> of your home. They would only be considered to be trespassing on private property, and (again) you cannot use deadly force to protect your property. Just ask Rodney Peairs, the guy who shot and killed the foreign exchange student, **Yoshihiro Hattori**, who went to the Peairs' house by mistake dressed up like John Travolta looking for the Halloween party in Baton Rouge, Louisiana in 1992. Even though Peairs was acquitted of manslaughter charges for shooting Yoshihiro after he rang the doorbell, Peairs was arrested, had to stand trial, was then sued in civil court (where the family was awarded $650k for the wrongful death of Yoshihiro) and he eventually felt compelled to apologize to the parents of Yoshihiro for killing their son by mistake. That is an awful lot of tragic forever pain for a lot of people because of a misunderstanding of your right to use deadly force.

Be careful not to use excessive force against someone who enters your home <u>but who is not attacking you</u>. They might believe they are in the right place! And if you don't think that could ever happen, just ask the family and friends of **Stephen Guillermo**. Stephen lived in a downtown San Francisco apartment building and came home one night after drinking in May, 2014. He accidentally got off the elevator on the wrong floor, and entered the wrong apartment (his was two stories up in the same spot). He was shot and killed by 68-year-old Amisi Sudi Kachepah, who was frightened by the unexpected intruder. No charges were eventually filed, but Kachepah was arrested, taken into custody, questioned, and now he has to live with the fact he killed some drunk guy going into the wrong apartment by mistake. There is also the classic example of "what if your daughter invited her boyfriend into the house without your knowledge?"

No one doubts the sanctity of our homes and property. We all have a right to feel safe in our homes, and there is no excuse for anyone entering our homes or trespassing on our property uninvited. But what is probably a brief, albeit horrific and terrifying encounter with a stranger in your home or on your property can become a nightmare that *never ends* if you let fear or over-zealous protective behavior guide your actions. Do yourself a favor and invest in locks, lights, cameras, and other security measures in addition to your gun—and only use your gun as a last resort when you have no other choice.

THE MOST IMPORTANT BEHAVIOR

CHOICE

Knowing what's unlawful is only the first step. One then has to *affirmatively* choose to *not* behave unlawfully!

Choice is the most powerful behavior we can exercise. While there are many things in life you cannot choose, YOU MOST CERTAINLY CAN CHOOSE TO BEHAVE LAWFULLY. Even if you don't actively make conscious choices about your behavior—your actions are your choices.

YOUR INTENT MATTERS! Simply, your intent is the reason why you did whatever it is you did—it is the actualization of your will. In the law, the level of punishment you get for committing an unlawful act is connected to the level of your intent for doing that act, with the highest penalties imposed when you act with purpose and intend your actions. This creates a deterrent to just going around and blatantly breaking the law, and it also allows for mitigating circumstances to count if you didn't really mean to do what you actually did.

A NOTE COMPARING ONE'S *WILL* TO ONE'S *INTENT:* There are conceptual nuances between one's will and one's intent. One's will is closer to one's personality or disposition, while one's intent refers specifically to one's state of mind at the time of a specific behavior or act. One's will is present whether or not one acts. And on a timeline, one's will comes before one behaves or acts. This note is important because one's will is never talked about in the law. The law does not pre-judge anyone based on any preconceived notions of personality or disposition, and focuses only on one's actions and their intent at the time of their actions (called *mens rea*). But since this is a book that requires the reader to think about their behavior well in advance of any actions they may take—I refer to one's will.

A NOTE ABOUT INTENT AND STRICT LIABILITY LAWS: Sometimes, your intent doesn't matter at all when you act, and you are automatically responsible for your actions just because you took those actions! It is called Strict Liability. This kind of liability is common for code violations, like in the vehicle code for traffic violations (because it doesn't matter if you meant to speed or not—it only matters that you did it). It also exists for certain situations where we need to be ultra-careful about our actions because the need is so important that you are required to take every precaution, like keeping wild animals or making sure you take great care when you do something dangerous. It is also in place for making sure the products you make for sale to the public are safe and making sure your sexual partner can give his or her consent, among others. This is important for you to know because you cannot get out of liability for your actions just by saying that you didn't mean your actions. Insincerity might allow you to get away with some shit sometimes or face a lower penalty for other shit other times—but not always!

SO HOW SHOULD YOU BEHAVE?

Luckily, there is no shortage of opinions on THAT! LOL! There is:

- **Religion:** Religion offers us a wonderful sense of community which can bring people together with a sense of oneness and belonging, following the sacred texts that have been handed down throughout the millennia. Just know that you are also expected to behave lawfully *in addition* to any faith you embrace. As it just so happens, only a couple of The Ten Commandments are actually still unlawful, only about 7% of the Mitzvot (from The Torah/Old Testament) is still found in the law, and an even smaller percentage of Islamic/Sharia Law reflects what is lawful in the United States today. What's important to realize is that the law today is a collage of the best ideas from the most influential minds throughout recorded history—including the sacred texts.

- **Secular Wisdom:** There is a wealth of wisdom out there that has been handed down throughout the ages found in inspirational quotes, adages, idioms, and other cultural sayings. These were all lessons that someone once learned that has been handed down so that others may also learn that lesson. <u>Let wisdom guide your behavior.</u> "*A bird in the hand is worth two in the bush*" is about certainty and risk; "*Never look a gift horse in the mouth*" is about gratitude; "*Don't take any wooden nickels*" is about understanding how the world actually works and not being taken advantage of; and "*Don't Sweat the Small Stuff*" is about acceptance and forgiveness—all valuable life lessons! And how many of us embrace the expression, "*Eat, Drink and be Merry, for tomorrow may never come,*" an expression that reminds us to enjoy life! Plus countless others!

- **Institutional or Professional Codes:** Just because certain wisdom became a slogan or a principle, that doesn't diminish its value. You should endeavor to "*First, Do No Harm*" when trying to help people (from the Hippocratic Oath of the medical profession), and you should "*Be All You Can Be*" (the US Army).

- **There are Archaic Laws and Codes:** While the 12th Century Code of Chivalry is often referred to as being dead, it involved honor, gallantry, service to others, and a certain respect and kindness toward women. But are those values really dead?

- **Service Organizations:** A Boy Scout is, '*Trustworthy, Loyal, Helpful, Friendly, Courteous, Kind, Obedient, Cheerful, Thrifty, Brave, Clean, and Reverent!*" What's wrong with any of that?

- **Personal Credos:** One of my favorite personal credos is from William Bourn, a successful California businessman at the turn of the last century who named his estate after his credo, which is now an historic landmark in Northern California: The FILOLI House, an acronym which stands for "*<u>Fi</u>ght for a just cause; <u>Lo</u>ve your fellow man; <u>Li</u>ve a good life.*" Pretty cool.

- **Personal Affirmations:** Growing up, my best friend Kenny's mom, Sandy, used to tell him to "Do good" every time she would say goodbye to him. I thought that was cool, it was a little different from what my mom used to tell me all the time, "Be good." My message would sometimes frustrate me because it felt like a miniature little lecture when I hadn't done anything wrong, when Kenny's message seemed to be a little message of empowerment. While I didn't realize it at the time, it was our moms using a sort of personal affirmation to remind us that <u>our behavior is a choice!</u> When I told this story years later to another friend, Sheelah, she laughed, saying she never heard of this, but said we were getting "momilies"—a homily from your mom, (probably after the book, "*Momilies*" by Michele Slung)—which made me laugh! But little messages said to loved ones become ingrained in our heads, and in later years become patterns of behavior and the affirmations we say to ourselves to stay positive and to succeed in life. (I love you, too, Mom. I'll try to be good.)

There are many ways to learn life's lessons:

LEARN FROM OTHER PEOPLE'S CHOICES:

I love *America's Funniest Home Videos*—I really do! All of those videos are little examples of what can go wrong and what not to do. I now avoid anything with wheels, usually hold the handrail (unless it's nasty), and I can now see that trampolines really are dangerous (thanks Dad, for insisting we didn't get one of those as kids). I can also see that spinning kids around and around and handing them a stick to swing wildly to try and hit the piñata without an ample clearing really isn't that good of an idea, either! Look around—there is no shortage of people doing stupid shit that you can learn from!

LEARN FROM CULTURE:

From music and film, to written and spoken word, painting, photography, sculpture, and all of the arts—artists and thinkers pour their hearts and souls into their work so that we may experience the beauty and pain of life through their vision, as they have created and still create the record of civilization—embrace it! Love it and live it! (By the way, this is the real value of a college education—learning how to appreciate culture, and learning how to think and express yourself by putting it all together as you develop your own worldview.)

LEARN THE BOUNDARIES OF ACCEPTABLE BEHAVIOR:

I think that the trick has always been to color within the lines—just like it was in grade school when you were learning how to color with crayons! You can color whatever you want and however you like (this represents your freedom), you just have to stay within the lines (this represents the law), as long as you do it in a way that doesn't harm or offend others (this is reasonableness).

My 6th grade teachers (Mrs. Calessa and Mrs. Thrasher) who used to yell at us non-stop every recess period, "You guys can do basically anything you want ...

we don't care what you do ... we have all these balls and all this playground equipment, an open grass area, even a baseball diamond ... why on earth would you choose to [*insert some stupid infraction here*]?!?" We used to laugh at Mrs. Calessa throwing her hands up and shaking her head with her big sunglasses showing us our reflections as she would yell at us. All these years later, I understand that they were trying to get us to learn and acknowledge the boundaries of acceptable behavior and to enjoy what was possible within those boundaries.

LEARN TO HAVE A HEALTHY RELATIONSHIP WITH POLICE / AUTHORITY:

I can't tell you how many times I've personally experienced getting a look down from a cop at a traffic intersection or while catching transit, and a simple nod of hello with a little smile on my part eased any tension or suspicion that may have existed (I guess I happen to look rather suspicious). With a simple gesture, I have been able to communicate time and time again that I acknowledge and accept the police presence. Sometimes, I even get a smile back!

LEARN TO FOLLOW THE PATH OF LEAST RESISTANCE:

This is one of the lessons my father always tried to teach us as kids: It's easier to just follow the law. It drove him nuts to see my mother leave the house at the absolute latest possible moment on her way somewhere (ironically, like going to church) forcing her to speed down the road in order to be on time, having us kids on the lookout for cops so that she wouldn't get a speeding ticket. In that circumstance, the path of least resistance is to just plan your time accordingly so that you don't have to speed down the road. Besides, having to always look out for police is exhausting! It starts to become a habit to look for them, and then you're always afraid of getting caught—even when you aren't doing anything wrong! It's just way easier to always be in compliance with the law and not give a shit if anyone is watching!

LEARN THE ART OF AVOIDANCE:

If you see a pile of shit, don't step in it! Never let anyone ever hand you a pile of shit, and if there is a pile of shit flying in your direction—DUCK!

LEARN FROM YOUR MISTAKES:

It is never too late to start living a lawful life. Penalties in our penal system are progressive (meaning they increase the next time), expressly for the purpose of allowing for redemption. Who gives a shit if you've fucked up a little in life? The important thing is to learn from your mistakes. If you have it in your mind that you are not a lawful person, you are not realizing your opportunity for redemption! Start fresh by living lawfully and feel the empowerment that comes from living a more wholesome, lawful life.

CLOSING THOUGHTS

I hope you have enjoyed this simplified tour of the fundamentals of American law through the examination of the preceding 20 human behaviors. And yes, I am fully aware that this book is completely oxymoronic: It is a list of rules to follow when the goal of American law has always been to protect us from the unlawful acts of others, NOT to establish some authoritarian code of conduct that could somehow infringe upon our natural freedoms. I am also aware of other problems with this book, too—primarily that this book is not well annotated with legal authorities or citations, and it is more of a casual delivery of ideas that I have accepted as my own from my lifelong education and my years of observation from countless sources that I could not begin to credit as I honestly have no idea where I first heard any ideas not my own. However, I believe this to be a book of elementary legal principles with easily verifiable truisms regarding information that is widely available and generally discussed openly and publicly.

That being said—the information inside of this book is what you need to know in order to live a lawful life in a free country. I believe that this basic and fundamental information is essential for every American to know and understand. I believe this information should be better integrated into our schools, our religious teachings, and taught throughout popular elements of our culture—including the evening news (I am so sick of hearing news correspondents butcher legal principles and legal theory in their presentation of the news). How can we be fully actualized members of society if we don't know the Rules of Lawful Behavior?

I'll even go so far as to say that I think The Rules of Lawful Behavior should become a standard addition to hotel rooms for visitors right along-side the Gideon Bible. Hell, there should be posters of the Rules of Lawful Behavior on billboards, at bus stops, and at train stations everywhere.

A NOTE ON RACISM AND THE LAW: There are claims that the law is (still) not being applied equally among racial groups in the United States, and that the law is being used to further racist motivations. It is sad to me that the best defense against these claims is, 'not always,' and then referring to some "bad apples in every bunch" idiom. We need to do better. It should not be about race, but about an individual's behavior and the law.

A NOTE ON PRIVILEGE: It seems to me that the main argument about privilege is not that the law is somehow flawed, but that law enforcement is so uneven and more harshly applied in certain circumstances, that it seems like there are classes of people not really subject to the law at all while others are overly scrutinized. YIKES! The argument shouldn't be about who should have to follow the law— everyone should have to follow the law! I'd rather see that everyone is taught to understand The Rules of Lawful Behavior and how to successfully navigate the law of the land, rather than to see state agents acting as arbitrators of some unsanctioned privilege.

A NOTE ON BIAS: I am not the first to acknowledge that a lot of what looks and feels like remnant institutional racism in our culture today is really a lot closer to the concept of personal bias (the assumptions we individually have already made about people or things in life, whether consciously or subconsciously). It can be said that to be biased about a group of people is half-way to being racist, sort of mid-point in a fucked-up continuum between non-racist and racist. Bias we actively engage and acknowledge would be called prejudice, which is a little further along on the continuum, and then we reach racist once the tiki-torches come out. The challenge before each of us is to understand and manage any biases we may have about people who look different from ourselves, and to not allow any biases we may have to interfere with how we treat and relate to people. In the immortal words of **Rodney King**, "Can't we all just get along?"

A NOTE TO ALL PARENTS: If you send your children off into the world without knowing the Rules of Lawful Behavior, then you are truly performing a disservice to your children and rolling the dice when it comes to their future. THEY ARE NOT TEACHING KIDS THIS INFORMATION IN SCHOOL. You do not want your children learning that their behavior was somehow unlawful by being told, "You have the right to remain silent." And you certainly do not want your children shot and killed because they didn't know how to act or respond to a situation that involves the police.

A NOTE TO PRIMARY AND HIGH SCHOOLS: You should implement The Rules of Lawful Behavior into your curricula. And if this expression of Lawful Behavior is too guttural, then I am happy to develop (or license for development) age appropriate material.

A NOTE TO JUDGES, LAWYERS, AND LAW SCHOOLS: If we perpetuate the idea that only the smartest and brightest among us are qualified to know and study the law, then we will never be able to maintain our free society as our population is growing so fast and so large. It's time to adopt more of a teaching role in our culture!

A NOTE TO ACTIVE MILITARY PERSONNEL: This book summarizes many essential American principles for which you are fighting for, and for which you have pledged your life to protect and preserve. I just thought you should know in case no one has told you yet.

A Message for Those Outside the Western World: It is my hope that my little treatise on American Law is a sort of message in a bottle that can help non-westerners better understand American/Western culture. It may very well be that all of this looks like absolute chaos from the outside, and the descriptor that "democracy is messy" may not be enough to allow one to easily make sense of it all (especially through the massive amounts of noise and the conspicuous consumption of our culture). And the politicians and bureaucrats who continue to work the system to their benefit may seem no different from any other tyrants in the world. But through common law principles of allowing the law to stand on its own, to live and to breathe as the law of the land, allowing legal principles to become well-established and known by all, we don't need to seek the approval from our leaders for our behavior. It is our system of justice that we expect to protect us from those who would do us harm, and from excessive government intrusion into our lives as we try to make sense of this precious gift of life that we have all been given. Most Americans believe that what we need to do is to preserve and protect our system of justice—only it is a lot trickier than it looks while seeking liberty and justice for all while facing the challenges of late modern post-industrialism, which now seems to include populist notions of hate and intolerance.

A Final Note about the Law and Morality: Just because there is no law that specifically forbids any certain behavior, that does not make that behavior right, reasonable, good, or appropriate. Only a douchebag tries to use the "there's no law against it" argument to try to justify their bad behavior. (Members of the Trump Administration come to mind.) While we keep trying to codify right, good, and appropriate behavior by making sets of regulations after sets of regulations, arguing endlessly over these regulations while some focus entirely on deregulation, I can't help thinking, can't we all just do the right thing? Even if there is no clear right thing, can't we just always do what's mostly right all of the time?

A Final Note to Everyone: When I was a kid it was a common expression to say that "life doesn't come with an instruction manual." Well, this isn't everything (by far), but here is some stuff you need to know.

Note Added at Time of Printing: As this book was going to print, we saw video of **George Floyd's** final moments of life with a Minneapolis police officer's knee on his neck. "I can't breathe" protests raged around our nation and the world, including a clash at the White House sending the President to an underground bunker. My thoughts kept racing to my previous question and I wondered:

Is this the incendiary event that will end up destroying this social experiment that we call Representative Democracy?

We clearly seem to have a police brutality problem in this country: Police are not supposed to kneel on the necks of anyone to the point of their death; police are not supposed to shoot non-violent fleeing felons in the back; police are not supposed to put people unrestrained in the back of vans and go joy-riding until they are dying from their injuries; and a hundred other despicable acts we seem to be seeing with more and more frequency. Let's hope this truly is a moment of change.